The Big Book *of* Table Toppers

The Big Book of Table Toppers
© 2017 by Martingale & Company®

Martingale®
19021 120th Ave. NE, Ste. 102
Bothell, WA 98011-9511 USA
ShopMartingale.com

Printed in China
22 21 20 19 18 17   8 7 6 5 4 3 2 1

Library of Congress Cataloging-in-Publication Data
is available upon request.

ISBN: 978-1-60468-848-1

MISSION STATEMENT

We empower makers who use fabric and yarn
to make life more enjoyable.

CREDITS

PUBLISHER AND
CHIEF VISIONARY OFFICER
Jennifer Erbe Keltner

CONTENT DIRECTOR
Karen Costello Soltys

DESIGN MANAGER
Adrienne Smitke

MANAGING EDITOR
Tina Cook

COVER AND TEXT DESIGNER
Regina Girard

ACQUISITIONS EDITOR
Karen M. Burns

PHOTOGRAPHER
Brent Kane

COPY EDITOR
Melissa Bryan

Contents

Introduction

Setting an inviting table is part of what makes a quilter's house a home. Whether it's a runner that shows off a dramatic centerpiece in the dining room, or a cozy kitchen table topper that rests beneath a bowl of fresh fruit, these versatile little quilts offer guests a glimpse of the hobby you love—quilting.

Though their descriptive name leads one to think, "I know exactly what to do with these quilts," don't let the moniker inhibit your creative use of these small quilts throughout your home. After all, they can look just as striking tucked into a cabinet or bookshelf beneath a collection of your favorite things, or draping off a cabinet front to add a pop of color in the corner of your family room.

Beyond the many places you can use and display them, table toppers and table runners have the added appeal of being projects you can start and finish in short order. And what's not to love about an array of small quilts that allows you to experiment with new-to-you techniques, dabble in appliqué, or revisit a favorite block pattern? Many scrappy table runners are perfect for using your stash or scrap bag full of leftover fabric bits and pieces.

So, what are you waiting for? There's a feast of ideas and inspiration awaiting you as you turn page after page! Our guess is that you'll find one or more for every season and every tabletop in your home. Enjoy.

Table Runners

Ranch String

String quilts have been stitched as make-do, use-it-up quilts for hundreds of years. They have historically been utilitarian quilts made from whatever scraps were available, usually strips or "strings" left over from other projects or from worn-out clothing. Instead of throwing away scraps, put your favorites to use in this beautiful and functional table runner.

FINISHED RUNNER: 13½" x 104½" • **FINISHED BLOCK:** 6½" x 6½"

Designed and made by Natalie Barnes; quilted by Angela Walters

Materials

Yardage is based on 42"-wide fabric.

3 yards *total* of assorted scraps for blocks

1¼ yards of accent fabric for blocks and binding

1⅝ yards of fabric for backing

20" x 111" piece of batting

Paper for foundation piecing

Cutting

From the accent fabric, cut:

4 rectangles, 10½" x 18"; crosscut into 32 strips, 2" x 10½"

7 strips, 2¼" x 42"

From the assorted scraps, cut:

150 strips, 1½" x 9"

150 strips, 1" x 9"

From the foundation paper, cut:

32 squares, 7" x 7"

MIX IT UP

While you can always use fat quarters and fat eighths, think of this project as a challenge to use your stash. Pull all of the fabrics from your scrap boxes as you sew, including anything that you may deem to be ugly or not matching. Put some unexpected colors in your blocks. Consider adding a Civil War–reproduction print or a 1970s-looking calico print. Mix up the scale of prints. You might even include some woven plaids or a shot cotton. What about an old linen tea towel? Linen calendar towels are fun to cut up and use in quilts. If you have a favorite multicolored print you'd like to use, look at the color windows or dots on the selvages to help you choose other fabrics. In short, mix things up and have fun doing it! Your project will be a real conversation piece at the dinner table.

Making the Blocks

By using your accent fabric in the same place—the diagonal center of the block—you'll be making blocks that you can then arrange to make a secondary pattern. For the quilt shown, the blocks were arranged to create a simple diamond. Before joining the blocks, take some time to try different layouts. Turn them and see what other designs you can make from this simple utilitarian block.

1 Place a 2" x 10½" strip of accent fabric right side up on a 7" square of foundation paper, positioning the strip on the diagonal from corner to corner. The strips will be longer than needed; you'll trim the ends even with the paper after you have covered the foundation with strips.

2 Choose a 9"-long strip from the assorted strips and place it right sides together with the accent-fabric strip, aligning the raw edges. Sew together with a ¼" seam allowance through all layers. Flip open and finger-press the seam allowances, or press with an iron.

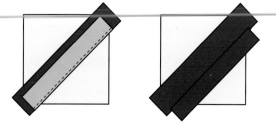

3 Repeat step 2 to add additional strips to each side of the accent strip, varying the strip widths and colors, until the entire 7" x 7" piece is covered. Trim your "strings" to shorter lengths as you approach the corners of the foundation square.

4 Repeat steps 1–3 until all 32 foundation squares have been covered with fabric strips.

Make 32.

5 Trim the blocks so that the strips are even with the 7"-square foundation. With right side up, press the blocks using spray sizing or spray starch. Note that if you use starch, you should be sure to wash your project once it's completed.

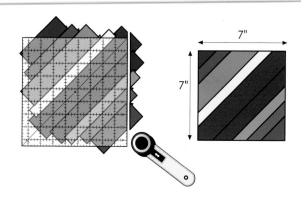

Assembling the Runner

1 Referring to the assembly diagram at right, arrange the blocks on a design wall or other flat surface, in 16 rows of two blocks each. Sew the blocks together in rows. Pin for accuracy, removing pins as you sew. Press the seam allowances in opposite directions from row to row. Sew the rows together, matching the block seam allowances and pinning for accuracy, to complete your runner top. Press the remaining seam allowances in one direction.

2 Stitch around the perimeter of the top a scant ¼" from the raw edges to keep seam allowances from coming unsewn and to prevent stretching or distortion of the blocks. The edges of the blocks are all cut on the bias and will stretch easily, so handle the top gently. Carefully remove the papers from the back of the blocks.

Finishing

Go to ShopMartingale.com/HowtoQuilt if you need more information on any of the finishing steps.

1 Layer, baste, and quilt your table runner.

2 Using the 2¼"-wide strips of accent fabric, prepare and attach the binding.

Quilt assembly

Grandma's Sewing Basket

Tammy grew up in the same farmhouse where her grandparents lived and her dad was raised. In a home chock-full of good memories, one of her favorites was of going through her grandma's sewing basket. Tammy used some of the treasures from that basket in this runner, as a tribute to her grandma.

FINISHED RUNNER: 19" x 49"

Designed and made by Tammy Johnson

Materials

Yardage is based on 42"-wide fabric.

- 1¼ yards of green print for outer border and binding
- ½ yard of light blue check for background*
- ½ yard of cream stripe for basket appliqués
- ¼ yard of gold wool or cotton for flower-petal appliqués
- ¼ yard of taupe plaid wool or cotton for flower-center appliqués
- ¼ yard of black print for inner border
- ⅛ yard of green wool or cotton for leaf appliqués
- Scrap, approximately 1½" x 18", of taupe solid wool or cotton for seed appliqués
- 1⅝ yards of fabric for backing
- 24" x 54" piece of batting
- 2 yards of ⅜"-wide ecru rickrack
- 6 assorted off-white buttons
- Fusible web (optional)

If your fabric is not at least 41½" wide after removing selvages, you'll need 1¼ yards.

Cutting

Using the patterns on page 15, prepare appliqué shapes from the fabrics indicated for your favorite method of appliqué. Tammy used fusible-web appliqué with machine stitching.

From the light blue check, cut:
1 rectangle, 11½" x 41½"

From the cream stripe, cut:
5 baskets*

From the gold wool or cotton, cut:
5 flower petals

From the taupe plaid wool or cotton, cut:
5 flower centers

From the green wool or cotton, cut:
10 leaves

From the taupe solid wool or cotton, cut:
15 seeds

From the black print, cut:
2 strips, 1¼" x 41½"**
2 strips, 1¼" x 13"

From the green print, cut on the lengthwise grain:
2 strips, 3½" x 43"
2 strips, 3½" x 19"
4 strips, 1½" x 42"

Vary the position of the basket pattern on the stripes to add interest.

**If your fabric is not wide enough, cut an extra strip and piece together for the needed length.*

Assembling the Runner

1 Fold the light blue check 11½" x 41½" rectangle in half to find the center. Make a light crease and position one of the basket appliqués over the center crease, placing it approximately ½" from the raw edge.

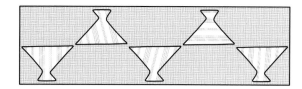

2 Position the remaining four baskets as shown. There should be approximately ⅜" between each basket. This is where the rickrack will be sewn. When you're happy with the placement of the baskets, appliqué them in place.

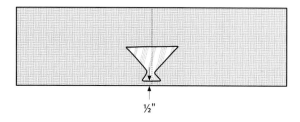

3 Position the flower petals and two leaves on each basket, tucking the ends of the leaves under the flowers. Vary the placement of flowers slightly for each basket. Next, position the flower centers. Finally, position three seed appliqués on each flower center. When you're happy with the placement, appliqué in place. Tammy stitched around the appliqué shapes with a machine blanket stitch and matching thread.

4 Position the rickrack, pinning it in place as you go. The rickrack curves should be approximately 4½" from the top edge of the baskets. Trim excess rickrack, and stitch in place with a machine straight stitch down the center of the rickrack.

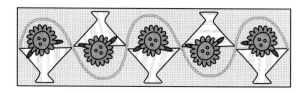

5 Sew the black print 1¼" x 41½" strips to the long sides of the table runner. Sew the black-print 1¼" x 13" strips to the short sides. Press.

6 Sew the green print 3½" x 43" strips to the long sides of the table runner. Stitch the green-print 3½" x 19" strips to the short sides. Press.

Finishing

Go to ShopMartingale.com/HowtoQuilt if you need more information on any of the finishing steps.

1 Layer, baste, and quilt your table runner.

2 Using the green print 1½"-wide strips, prepare and attach the binding. (Tammy used single-fold binding, not double-fold.)

3 Sew on the six off-white buttons, one at each basket corner.

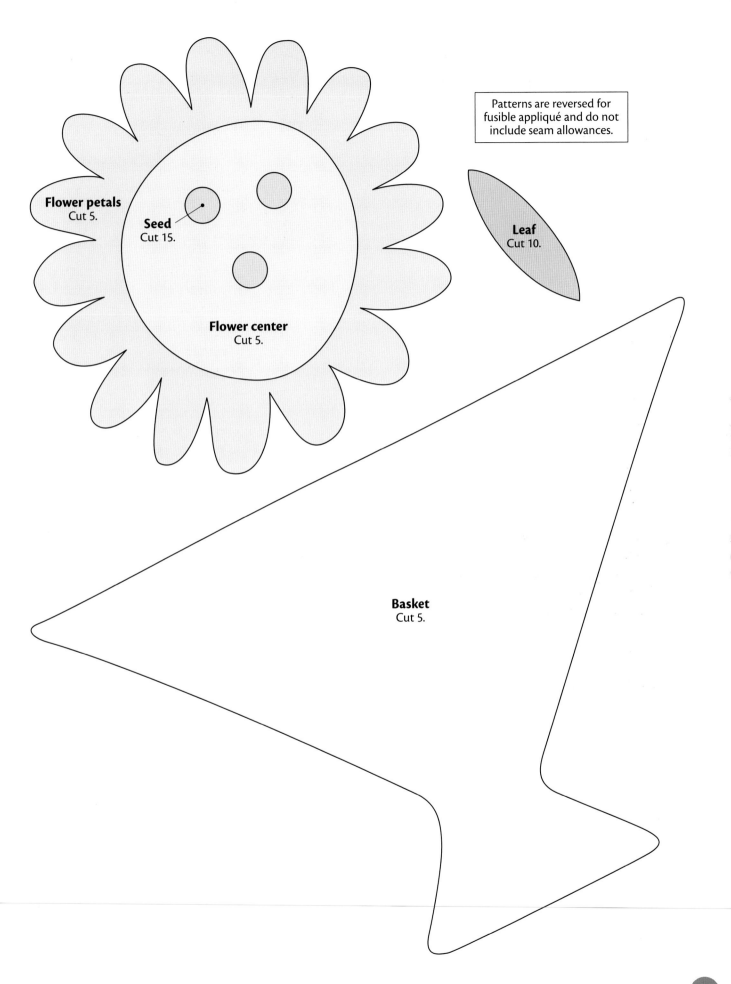

Patterns are reversed for fusible appliqué and do not include seam allowances.

Flower petals
Cut 5.

Seed
Cut 15.

Leaf
Cut 10.

Flower center
Cut 5.

Basket
Cut 5.

Calamity Cross

The block in this table runner was the result of random experimentation. Jenifer made a simple bordered-square block, sliced it in two, and added a darker strip. She then cut it in two again and added a second strip to make a cross. Voilà! The result is a fun block, without the fuss of cutting and sewing lots of small pieces.

FINISHED RUNNER: 12" x 72" • **FINISHED BLOCK:** 6" x 6"
Designed and made by Jenifer Dick

Materials

Yardage is based on 42"-wide fabric.

2¼ yards of yellow solid for blocks, background, binding, and backing

¼ yard of cream solid for blocks

¼ yard of dark gold solid for blocks

18" x 78" piece of batting

Cutting

From the yellow solid, cut on the *lengthwise* grain:

1 strip, 5½" x 72½"
1 strip, 1½" x 72½"
1 strip, 18" x 78"
3 strips, 2" x 72"

From the remainder of the yellow solid, cut on the *crosswise* grain:

10 rectangles, 1½" x 3½"
12 rectangles, 1½" x 6½"
10 rectangles, 2½" x 3½"
15 rectangles, 2½" x 6½"

From the cream solid, cut:

10 squares, 3½" x 3½"

From the dark gold solid, cut:

20 strips, 1" x 6½"

Making the Blocks

1 Sew a yellow 1½" x 3½" rectangle to the top edge of a cream square. Sew a yellow 2½" x 3½" rectangle to the bottom edge of the square. Press the seam allowances toward the rectangles.

2 Sew a yellow 2½" x 6½" rectangle to the right side of the unit. Sew a yellow 1½" x 6½" rectangle to the left side of the unit. Press the seam allowances toward the rectangles.

3 Measure and cut 2¾" from the left side of the assembled unit. Sew a dark gold strip between the pieces of the unit. Press the seam allowances toward the strip.

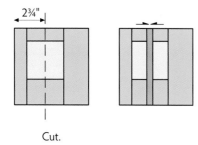

Cut.

● SEWING THE BLOCKS

When inserting the dark gold strips, align the horizontal seamlines in the two sections and pin. The units can easily become skewed and will look wonky without care.

4 Rotate the unit 90°, positioning the dark gold strip near the bottom edge, and cut again, 2¾" from the left side. Sew a dark gold strip between the two pieces of the block. Press the seam allowances toward the dark gold strip. Make 10, keeping the orientation of the pieced units the same when making each cut.

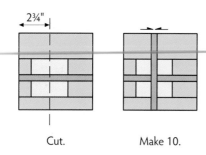

Cut.   Make 10.

● CREATIVE CROSSES

To add interest to the table runner, Jenifer varied the measurements when she sliced the units before inserting the dark gold strips. Use the photograph on page 16 as a guide to duplicate her free-form design, or cut all the units as directed for a more uniform appearance.

Assembling the Runner

1 Lay out the 10 blocks and the remaining yellow 6½" rectangles as shown or as desired. Rotate some blocks to vary the cross placement.

2 Sew the blocks and rectangles together in a row and press. The row should measure 6½" x 72½".

3 Sew the yellow 5½" x 72½" strip to one long edge of the pieced row. Sew the yellow 1½" x 72½" strip to the other long edge. Press the seam allowances toward the strips.

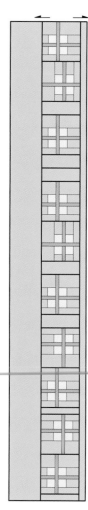

Table-runner
assembly

Finishing

Go to ShopMartingale.com/HowtoQuilt if you need more information on any of the finishing steps.

1 Layer, baste, and quilt your table runner.

2 Using the yellow 2"-wide strips, prepare and attach the binding.

Birds of a Feather

This crisp and cheery table runner can easily be adjusted to fit any table by adding additional rows of geese. For an extra layer of functionality, use a piece of insulated batting along with the cotton batting when you quilt the runner so that you can put hot serving dishes directly on it without harming your table.

FINISHED RUNNER: 12½" x 44"
Designed and made by Melissa Lunden

Materials
Yardage is based on 42"-wide fabric.

1 yard of white solid linen for background and binding

⅛ yard *each* of dusty blue, light blue, dark gray, navy, rose, and yellow solid linen for flying-geese units

1½ yards of fabric for backing

16" x 47" piece of cotton batting

16" x 47" piece of insulated batting (optional)

Cutting

From the white solid linen, cut:
1 strip, 12½" x 42"; crosscut into:
    3 rectangles, 6½" x 12½"
    2 rectangles, 3¼" x 12½"
    2 rectangles, 1½" x 12½"
5 strips, 2" x 42"; crosscut into 96 squares, 2" x 2"
3 strips, 2½" x 42"

From *each* colored linen, cut:
8 rectangles, 2" x 3½" (48 total)

Assembling the Runner

1 Draw a diagonal line on the wrong side of each white 2" square.

2 Position a marked square on one end of a dusty blue 2" x 3½" rectangle, right sides together. Sew on the marked line. Trim the excess fabric ¼" from the stitching line. Press the seam allowances open. Repeat on the opposite end of the rectangle to make a flying-geese unit. Make a total of eight dusty blue flying-geese units.

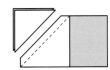

Make 8.

3 Repeat step 2 with the remaining marked white squares and the light blue, dark gray, navy, rose, and yellow rectangles to make a total of 48 flying-geese units.

4 Select eight flying-geese units in assorted colors. Sew the units together in a column with all of the units pointing in the same direction as shown. Press the seam allowances open. Make six columns.

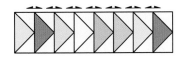

Make 6.

5 Refer to the assembly diagram at right to arrange the flying-geese columns and the white rectangles as shown. Sew the pieces together. Press the seam allowances open.

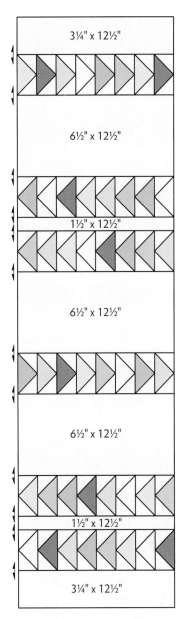

3¼" x 12½"

6½" x 12½"

1½" x 12½"

6½" x 12½"

6½" x 12½"

1½" x 12½"

3¼" x 12½"

Table-runner assembly

Finishing

Go to ShopMartingale.com/HowtoQuilt if you need more information on any of the finishing steps.

1 Layer the table-runner top with backing and cotton batting. If you're using the insulated batting, layer it between the cotton batting and the table-runner top, reflective side up. Baste the layers together; quilt.

2 Using the white 2½"-wide strips, prepare and attach the binding.

Rainy Day

Amber became inspired by a little doodle in one of her sketchbooks. Each trio of raindrops was originally scribbled into the corner of a big empty block separated by sashing. After preparing all the raindrop appliqués, she discovered that they formed raindrop medallions when brought closer together. This slightly sophisticated table runner is sure to bring some sunshine to your rainy days!

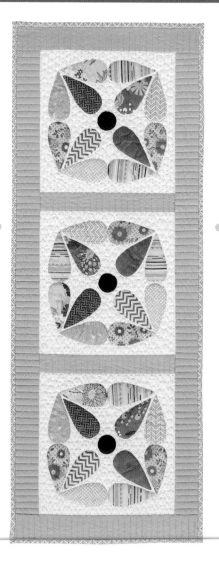

FINISHED RUNNER: 16" x 42" • **FINISHED BLOCK:** 11½" x 11½"

Designed and made by Amber Johnson; quilted by Natalia Bonner

Materials

Yardage is based on 42"-wide fabric.

½ yard of cream polka dot for block backgrounds

⅜ yard of blue solid for border and sashing

10" x 10" square *each* of 4 assorted red prints for raindrop appliqués

10" x 10" square *each* of 4 assorted gold prints for raindrop appliqués

10" x 10" square *each* of 4 assorted blue prints for raindrop appliqués

5" x 5" square of navy solid for circle appliqués

⅜ yard of blue-and-cream print for binding

1½ yards of fabric for backing

24" x 46" piece of batting

Freezer paper (optional)

Basting glue

Cutting

From the cream polka dot, cut:
3 squares, 12" x 12"

From the blue solid, cut:
2 strips, 2" x 12"
2 strips, 2½" x 38"
2 strips, 2½" x 16"

From the blue-and-cream print, cut:
4 strips, 2½" x 42"

● FABRIC FRUGALITY

You can use the same fabric for the backing and the block backgrounds if you'd like to minimize your fabric purchases. Buy 1½ yards of fabric, and then cut a 24" x 46" piece on the lengthwise grain for the backing and three 12" squares from the remaining fabric for the blocks.

Appliquéing the Blocks

Appliqué patterns for the raindrop and circle are below. Amber used freezer-paper appliqué with machine stitching, but you can prepare the shapes for your favorite method. For more information on machine appliqué, go to ShopMartingale.com/HowtoQuilt.

1 Prepare three appliqué raindrops from each of the red, gold, and blue prints (36 total). Prepare three appliqué circles from the navy solid.

2 Fold and press a cream 12" square in half vertically, horizontally, and on both diagonals to make creases for aligning the appliqué pieces. Place one raindrop from each print and one navy circle onto the background square as shown, glue basting if desired and leaving a 1" outer margin around the appliqués. Prepare three blocks.

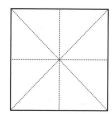

Press creases.

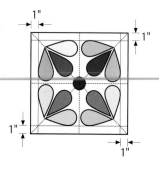

3 Appliqué the shapes into position. If you wish, machine appliqué around the raindrops and circles using a hem or zigzag stitch and invisible thread. Be sure to set your machine's settings back to normal when finished. If necessary, use the tip of a straight pin to tuck any exposed seam allowances back under the points of the raindrops while you're machine appliquéing.

Assembling the Runner

1 Sew together the three appliqué blocks and two blue 2" x 12" strips in alternating positions. Press the seam allowances toward the blue strips.

2 Pin and sew the blue 2½" x 38" strips to the long sides of the table-runner top. Pin and sew the blue 2½" x 16" strips to the short sides. Press all seam allowances toward the blue border.

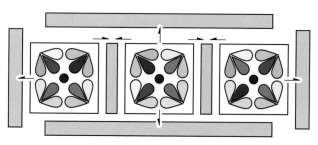

Table-runner assembly

Finishing

Go to ShopMartingale.com/HowtoQuilt if you need more information on any of the finishing steps.

1 Layer, baste, and quilt your table runner.

2 Using the blue-and-cream 2½"-wide strips, prepare and attach the binding.

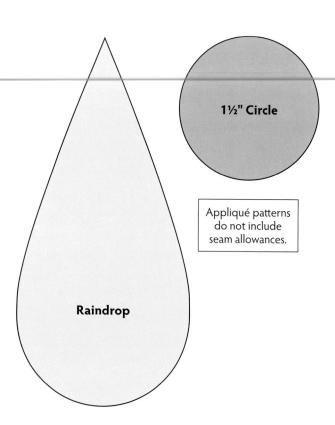

1½" Circle

Raindrop

Appliqué patterns do not include seam allowances.

Rosy

On a rare visit by Londoner Kaffe Fassett to the Pennsylvania home and studio of Liza Prior Lucy, the design partners decided to revisit a popular classic—the Nine Patch. Liza stresses that this is a scrap quilt, and encourages quiltmakers to "place the fabrics any which way…it isn't possible to do it wrong!"

FINISHED RUNNER: 18½" x 72½"

Designed and made by Kaffe Fassett and Liza Prior Lucy; quilted by Judy Irish

Materials

Yardage is based on 42"-wide fabric.

1 yard *total* of assorted small- to medium-scale prints for Nine Patch blocks

⅔ yard *total* of assorted large-scale prints for plain squares

¼ yard of very large-scale floral for plain squares*

½ yard of dotted print for binding

2⅓ yards of fabric for backing

22" x 76" piece of batting

Yardage may vary depending upon fabric repeat.

Cutting

From the small- to medium-scale prints, cut a *total* of:
162 squares, 2½" x 2½"*

From the very large-scale floral, fussy cut:
4 squares, 6½" x 6½"**

From the assorted large-scale prints, cut a *total* of:
14 squares, 6½" x 6½"

From the dotted print, cut:
5 strips, 2¼" x 42"

*Cut these squares in 18 assorted sets of 5 matching squares and 18 assorted sets of 4 matching squares.

**Center the very large-scale floral motif in each square.

● CUT EXTRAS AND PLAY!

Cut a few extra 6½" and 2½" squares to allow for optimum flexibility in arranging the fabrics and colors.

Making the Blocks

Arrange five matching 2½" small- or medium-scale print squares and four matching 2½" squares cut from a different small- or medium-scale print as shown. Strive for a pleasing balance of colors. Sew the squares into rows; press. Pin and stitch the rows together, carefully matching and nesting the seam allowances for accuracy; press. Make 18 Nine Patch blocks.

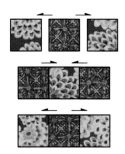
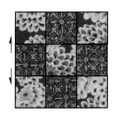

Make 18.

BE UNPREDICTABLE

Here and there, replace one 2½" print square with one cut from another fabric. Such intentional "errors" add surprise and charm to your piece and enable the prints and colors to blend better throughout the quilt.

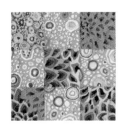

Assembling the Runner

1 Arrange the fussy-cut 6½" squares, the large-scale print 6½" squares, and the Nine Patch blocks in 12 horizontal rows of three squares or blocks each, alternating them as shown in the assembly diagram at right. Take time to rearrange the squares and blocks, scattering the fussy-cut blocks and colors evenly.

2 Sew the blocks together into rows; press.

3 Pin and sew the rows together, carefully matching the seam allowances; press.

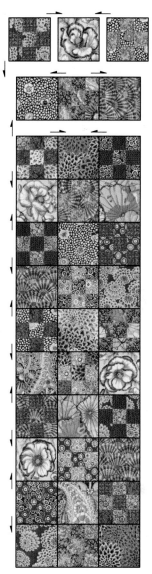

Assembly diagram

Finishing

Go to ShopMartingale.com/HowtoQuilt if you need more information on any of the finishing steps.

1 Layer, baste, and quilt your table runner.

2 Using the dotted 2¼"-wide strips, prepare and attach the binding.

A Pack of Posies

Make this table runner in no time at all with one charm pack and a half yard of fabric. The flowers and leaves are symmetrical, and the patterns can be used for either fusible-web or hand appliqué. Choose your favorite method and off you go!

FINISHED RUNNER: 17" x 51" • **FINISHED BLOCK:** 6" x 6"
Designed and made by Vicki Bellino

Materials

Yardage is based on 42"-wide fabric. Charm squares are 5" x 5".

36 charm squares of assorted medium/dark prints in blue, green, orange, red, and tan for patchwork blocks and appliqués
½ yard of light print for appliqué background and setting triangles
¼ yard of red print for binding
1½ yards of fabric for backing*
19" x 54" piece of batting
Fusible web (optional)

*If you don't mind piecing the backing, purchase 1⅛ yards.

Cutting

Using the patterns on page 31, prepare appliqué shapes from the fabrics indicated for your favorite method of appliqué. Vicki used fusible-web appliqué; for details, go to ShopMartingale.com/ HowtoQuilt for downloadable information. Set aside 6 light and 6 medium/dark charm squares before cutting.

From the light print, cut:
2 squares, 9¾" x 9¾"; cut each square into quarters diagonally to yield 8 triangles
4 squares, 6½" x 6½"

From *each of 12* medium/dark charm squares, cut:
2 rectangles, 2½" x 4½" (24 total)

From *each of 3* medium/dark charm squares, cut:
4 squares, 2½" x 2½" (12 total)

From *each of 4* medium/dark charm squares, cut:
1 large and 1 medium circle (4 total of each)

From 1 medium charm square, cut:
4 small circles

From 1 green charm square, cut:
4 stems

From *each of 3* green charm squares, cut:
8 leaves (24 total)

From the red print, cut:
3 strips, 2" x 42"

Making the Blocks

1 Draw a diagonal line on the wrong side of the six light 5" squares you've set aside. With right sides together, place one light square on top of each of the medium/dark 5" squares and sew ¼" from each side of the drawn line. Cut apart on the drawn line to make a total of 12 half-square-triangle units. Press the seam allowances toward the darker fabrics. Square up each unit to 4½" x 4½".

Make 12.

2 Stitch a medium/dark 2½" x 4½" rectangle to a light side of each half-square-triangle unit from step 1 as shown. Press the seam allowances toward the rectangle.

3 Sew a medium/dark 2½" square to one end of each remaining medium/dark 2½" x 4½" rectangle. Press the seam allowances toward the rectangle. Stitch these units to the remaining light side of the units from step 2. Press. Make 12 blocks. Your blocks should measure 6½" x 6½".

Make 12.

4 Center a prepared stem, six leaves, and one each of the large, medium, and small circles on each of the four light 6½" squares. Appliqué in place.

Make 4.

Assembling the Runner

1 Lay out the patchwork blocks, appliquéd blocks, and setting triangles as shown, with the flower stems all pointing toward the center. If you want to achieve the same look as the table runner pictured, pay careful attention to the orientation of the patchwork blocks.

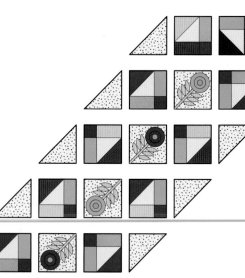

2 Once you're satisfied with the arrangement, sew the blocks and setting triangles together in rows as shown. Press the seam allowances in opposite directions from row to row. Sew the rows together and press.

Finishing

Go to ShopMartingale.com/HowtoQuilt if you need more information on any of the finishing steps.

1 Layer, baste, and quilt your table runner.

2 Using the red 2"-wide strips, prepare and attach the binding.

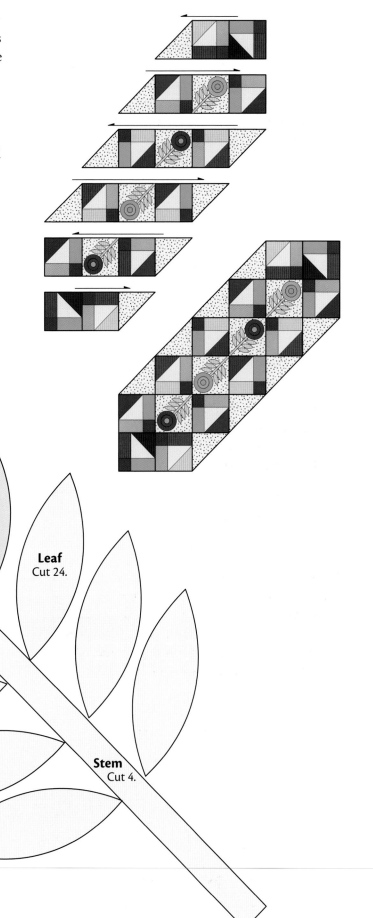

Large circle
Cut 4.

Medium circle
Cut 4.

Small circle
Cut 4.

Leaf
Cut 24.

Stem
Cut 4.

Patterns do not include seam allowances.

Peppermint Candy

This bright, cheerful table runner features pieced Pinwheel blocks that look like peppermint candies. Using different red and green fabrics gives each block its own personality and helps use up some of your stash. This runner is so easy, you may just want to make several to have on hand for last-minute holiday gifts.

FINISHED RUNNER: 11½" x 35½" • **FINISHED BLOCK:** 6" x 6"

Designed and made by Cheryl Almgren Taylor; quilted by Cheryl Winslow

Materials

Yardage is based on 42"-wide fabric.

⅔ yard of green print for middle border and binding

⅝ yard of white print for blocks and pieced inner and outer borders

⅓ yard of red dot for blocks and pieced inner and outer borders

¼ yard *total* of assorted green prints for blocks

¼ yard *total* of assorted red prints for blocks

⅝ yard of fabric for backing

16" x 40" piece of batting

Cutting

From the white print, cut:

10 squares, 3" x 3"

4 strips, 2½" x 21"; crosscut *1 strip* into 8 squares, 1½" x 1½"

From the assorted red prints, cut a *total* of:

9 squares, 3" x 3"

From the assorted green prints, cut a *total* of:

5 pairs of squares, 3⅞" x 3⅞"; cut each square in half diagonally to yield 20 triangles

From the red dot, cut:

1 square, 3" x 3"

4 strips, 2½" x 21"; crosscut *1 strip* into 8 rectangles, 1½" x 2"

From the green print for middle border and binding, cut:

3 strips, 1" x 42"; crosscut into:

    2 strips, 1" x 32½"

    2 strips, 1" x 9½"

2½"-wide bias strips to total 104" in length

Making the Blocks

1 Using a pencil and ruler, draw a diagonal line from corner to corner on the wrong side of the white 3" squares. Place a marked white square on top of each assorted red and red dot 3" square, right sides together. Sew ¼" from both sides of the marked line. Cut the squares apart on the drawn line and press the seam allowances toward the red. Each pair of squares will make two half-square-triangle units.

Make 20.

2 Sew two different half-square-triangle units together as shown. Repeat to make a total of 10 pairs. Sew 2 pairs together to make a block center. Repeat to make a total of five block centers. Press the seam allowances toward the red triangles.

Make 5.

3 Sew four matching green triangles to the sides of each block center, adding opposite sides first. Press the seam allowances toward the triangles. The blocks should measure 6½" x 6½".

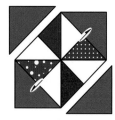 

Make 5.

Assembling the Runner

1 Sew the blocks together side by side. Press the seam allowances toward the second and fourth blocks. The runner top must measure 6½" x 30½" for the pieced borders to fit properly.

2 To make the pieced inner border, sew a red dot 2½" x 21" strip to each long side of a white 2½" x 21" strip to make strip set A. Sew a white 2½" x 21" strip to each long side of a red dot 2½" x 21" strip to make strip set B. Press the seam allowances toward the red. Crosscut each strip set into 12 segments, 1½" wide.

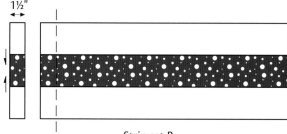

Strip set A.
Make 1. Cut 12 segments.

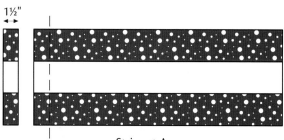

Strip set B.
Make 1. Cut 12 segments.

3 Sew together three A segments and two B segments, alternating them as shown on page 35. Press the seam allowances toward the A segments. Repeat to make a total of two strips. Sew the strips to the long edges of the runner top. Press the seam allowances toward the borders. Sew a white 1½" square to each end of two A segments. Press the seam allowances toward

the A segments. Add these border strips to the short edges of the runner top. Press the seam allowances toward the borders.

Sew the green 1" x 32½" strips to the long edges of the runner top. Press the seam allowances toward the green borders. Sew the green 1" x 9½" strips to the short edges of the runner top. Press the seam allowances toward the green borders. The runner top must now measure 9½" x 33½" for the pieced outer border to fit properly.

Join three B segments and two A segments end to end, alternating them. Add a red dot 1½" x 2" rectangle to each end of the strip. Press the seam allowances toward the A segments and the red dot rectangles. Repeat to make a total of two strips. Sew these strips to the long edges of the runner top. Press the seam allowances toward the green middle border. Sew a red dot 1½" x 2"

rectangle and then a white 1½" square to each end of the remaining two B segments. Press the seam allowances toward the red rectangles. Add these strips to the short edges of the table-runner top. Press the seam allowances toward the green middle border.

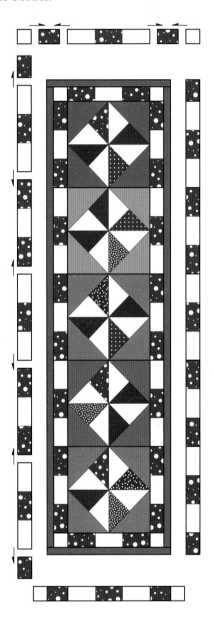

Finishing

Go to ShopMartingale.com/HowtoQuilt if you need more information on any of the finishing steps.

1 Layer, baste, and quilt your table runner.

2 Using the green print 2½"-wide strips, prepare and attach the bias binding.

Summer Picnic

Ordinarily Laurie Shifrin looks to Mother Nature as her muse, but she reports that a bag of colorful plastic drinking straws in blues and greens generated the idea for this table runner. Slender strips of folded batik fabrics are inserted into the seams of the classic Rail Fence block, and although these strips are pressed flat, they certainly convey the original—and unusual— inspiration.

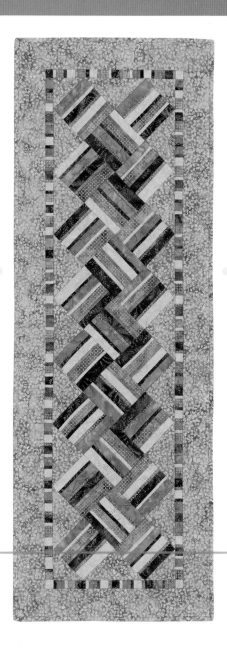

FINISHED RUNNER: 17⅞" x 51¾"
Designed and made by Laurie Shifrin

Materials

Yardage is based on 42"-wide fabric.

1¾ yards of floral batik for setting triangles, outer border, and binding

⅜ yard *each* of lime green, blue, turquoise, and navy batik for blocks and pieced inner border

1¾ yards of fabric for backing

22" x 56" piece of batting

Cutting

From *each* lime green, blue, turquoise, and navy batik, cut:
3 strips, 1" x 42" (12 total)
4 strips, 1½" x 42" (16 total)

From the remaining yardage of the lime green, blue, turquoise, and navy batiks, cut a *total* of:
3 strips, 1" x 20"
3 strips, 1½" x 20"

From the floral batik, cut on the *lengthwise* grain:
3 strips, 2¾" x 56"
3 strips, 2¼" x 56"

From the remaining floral batik, cut:
4 squares, 7" x 7"; cut each square into quarters diagonally to yield 16 triangles
2 squares, 3¾" x 3¾"; cut each square in half diagonally to yield 4 triangles

Making the Blocks

1 Fold each lime green, blue, turquoise, and navy 1" x 42" strip in half lengthwise; press. (With batik fabric, there's no need to worry about folding with a certain side facing out—both sides are the right side!) Make 12.

2 Align the raw edges of a folded strip along the long edge of a different-colored 1½" x 42" batik strip. Machine baste the two strips together with a ³⁄₁₆" seam allowance as shown. Make 12 scrappy combinations, three using each color of the 1½" x 42" strips. Press the seam allowances flat.

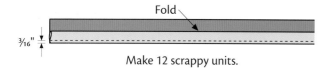

Fold

³⁄₁₆"

Make 12 scrappy units.

3 Cut each unit from step 2 and each remaining 1½" x 42" batik strip in half crosswise to yield two 1½" x 21" units/strips. Sort the units and strips into eight groups of three scrappy units and one contrasting 1½"-wide batik strip.

4 Reset your sewing machine to a regular stitch length (10 to 12 stitches per inch). Working one group at a time, arrange and sew the three units and one batik strip together along their long edges to make a flanged strip set as shown. Press, taking care to keep the folded edges flat and smooth. Make eight strip sets. Crosscut each strip set into three 4½" blocks (24 total). Set the remaining portions aside for the pieced inner border.

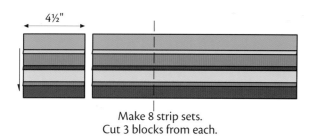

4½"

Make 8 strip sets.
Cut 3 blocks from each.

Assembling the Runner

1 Arrange the blocks, the floral quarter-square side setting triangles, and the floral half-square corner setting triangles in diagonal rows, alternating the orientation of the strips (horizontal versus vertical) as shown in the assembly diagram. Rearrange the blocks as necessary to achieve a pleasing color balance. You will have one block left over; set this aside for another project.

2 Sew the blocks and side setting triangles together in diagonal rows. Press, taking care to keep the folded edges smooth and flat.

3 Pin and then sew the rows together, carefully matching the seam allowances for accuracy. Add the corner setting triangles; press.

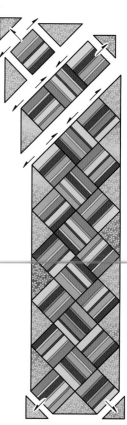

Assembly diagram

Adding the Borders

1 Use the three 1" x 20" batik strips and the three 1½" x 20" batik strips to make a strip set with folded inserts as described in "Making the Blocks" on page 38. Note that this strip set does not include the extra 1½"-wide batik strip.

2 Use a seam ripper to remove the plain 1½"-wide batik strip from each remaining strip-set segment from "Making the Blocks." Crosscut these strip-set segments and the strip set you made in step 1 into a total of 40 segments, 1¼" wide. Stitch the segments together end to end in random order to make one long strip. Make sure all the folded inserts face the same direction.

1¼"

Cut 40 segments.

3 Measure the length of the runner top through the center. Use a seam ripper to remove a portion of the long pieced strip equal to this measurement, adjusting as necessary to avoid having the ends of the new strip fall on a folded

insert. Make two. Pin and sew one pieced strip to each long side of the runner. Press the seam allowances toward the center of the quilt top.

4 Measure the width of the runner top through the center, including the borders just added. Repeat step 3 to separate, pin, and sew a pieced border strip to each short side of the runner; press.

5 Measure the length of the runner through the center. Trim two 2¾"-wide floral outer-border strips to this length. Pin and sew one strip to each long side of the runner. Press the seam allowances toward the newly added border.

6 Measure the width of the runner through the center, including the borders just added. Repeat step 5 to trim, pin, and sew a 2¾"-wide floral outer-border strip to each short side of the runner; press.

Finishing

Go to ShopMartingale.com/HowtoQuilt if you need more information on any of the finishing steps.

1 Layer, baste, and quilt your table runner.

2 Using the floral 2¼"-wide strips, prepare and attach the binding.

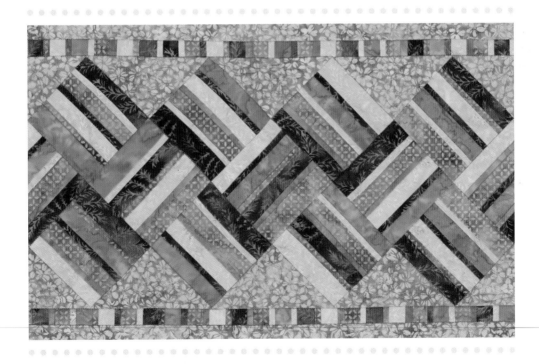

Confetti

A sprinkling of confetti is a fun way to add zing to a birthday or any happy occasion. But it is messy. Natalie decided to make her own version in the form of a runner that could transform a table into a celebration any time of year—and it's so much easier to clean up than the real thing!

FINISHED RUNNER: 12" x 72" • **FINISHED BLOCK:** 12" x 12"
Designed and made by Natalie Barnes

Materials

Yardage is based on 42"-wide fabric. Fat quarters are 18" x 21".

17 strips, 2½" x 42", of assorted dark prints in purple, green, and burgundy for blocks
3 fat quarters OR 6 strips, 2½" x 42", of assorted bright-orange or red accent prints for blocks
⅜ yard of purple batik for binding
1¼ yards of fabric for backing
18" x 78" piece of batting

Cutting

From 12 of the assorted dark strips, cut a *total* of:
162 squares, 2½" x 2½"

From the 5 remaining dark strips:
Trim each strip to 1½" x 42"; crosscut a total of 108 squares, 1½" x 1½"

From *each of the 3* bright accent prints, cut:
1 strip, 2½" x 21"; crosscut a total of 18 squares, 2½" x 2½"
2 strips, 1½" x 21"; crosscut a total of 36 squares, 1½" x 1½"

From the purple batik, cut:
5 strips, 2" x 42"

● LET THE FABRIC
DO THE WORK

The seemingly random design in this runner is constructed from four-patch units incorporated into Nine Patch blocks. The "confetti" is all in the color placement, so choose brightly saturated fabrics with high contrast.

● FLEXIBLE
PLACEMENT

If desired, make extra four-patch units to allow flexibility for creating completely random blocks. Use the leftover pieces to make coordinating coasters.

Making the Blocks

Each 12½" x 12½" block is composed of nine four-patch units, and each four-patch unit includes one piece of bright accent print for confetti. There are three different four-patch layouts, designated blocks A, B, and C; you'll make 18 of each. To prepare for piecing the blocks, stack the fabrics by your sewing area.

1 Lay out a small four-patch unit using three dark 1½" squares and one bright 1½" square. Sew the squares together in two rows. In the row with one bright and one dark square, press the seam allowances toward the dark fabric; in the row with two dark squares, press the seam allowances in the other direction so that the seams will nest together. Repeat to make 36 four-patch units.

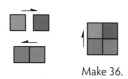

Make 36.

2 To make block A, join one small four-patch unit and three assorted dark 2½" squares as shown. Repeat to make 18 of block A. Press. The blocks should measure 4½" x 4½".

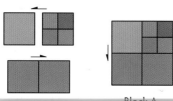

Block A.
Make 18.

3 To make block B, join one small four-patch unit and three assorted dark 2½" squares as shown. This is similar to block A, but the placement of the bright square is different. Press. Repeat to make 18 of block B. The blocks should measure 4½" x 4½".

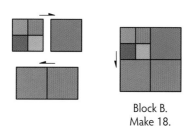

Block B.
Make 18.

4 To make block C, join three assorted dark 2½" squares and one bright 2½" square as shown. Make 18 of block C. The blocks should measure 4½" x 4½".

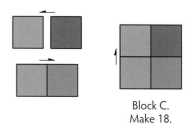

Block C.
Make 18.

5 Arrange blocks A, B, and C as shown, placing the A blocks in the left column, the B blocks in the right column, and the C blocks in the center. Rotate the blocks as needed to correctly position the four-patch units.

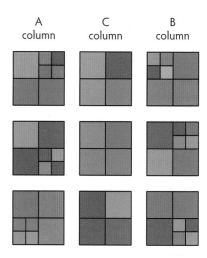

6 Sew the A, B, and C blocks together in rows, matching all seam intersections. Pin for accuracy, removing pins as you sew. Press. Sew the three rows together to complete the 12½" Nine Patch block. Make six.

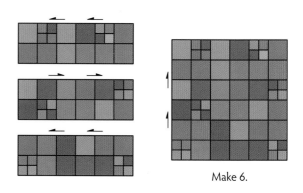

Make 6.

Assembling the Runner

Lay out the six large blocks as shown, rotating each block 90° from the previous block to create the random effect shown in the sample table runner. When you're satisfied with the layout, sew the blocks together and press the seam allowances in one direction.

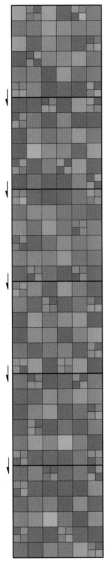

Table-runner assembly

Finishing

Go to ShopMartingale.com/HowtoQuilt if you need more information on any of the finishing steps.

1. Layer, baste, and quilt your table runner.

2. Using the purple 2"-wide strips, prepare and attach the binding.

● CHOOSING A QUILTING MOTIF

When looking for a quilting motif, Natalie often goes right to the fabric in the quilt. The zigzag quilting that completes her table runner came directly from one of the batiks she used. Another handy tip: Use any leftover blocks from your runner to test the quilting motif, thread colors, and tension. This gives you a chance to make sure you like your choices before quilting the finished project.

Simply Simple

Cindy designed a runner for a local quilt shop and called it Simply Simple. It was a tremendously popular pattern because it was, well, simple. Here, she's pared down the design even more and left the ends without a border treatment so that you can easily tailor the length to your own table. Couldn't be simpler!

FINISHED RUNNER: 15½" x 38½"
Designed and made by Cindy Lammon

Materials

Yardage is based on 42"-wide fabric.

⅓ yard of large-scale print for center

¼ yard of white solid for inner and outer borders

⅛ yard of red solid for pieced middle border

4" x 12" rectangle *each* of 5 green and/or gray prints for pieced middle border

⅓ yard of green print for binding

⅔ yard of fabric for backing*

20" x 42" piece of batting

*If the backing fabric doesn't measure 42" wide after it's been washed, you'll need 1⅓ yards.

Cutting

From the red solid, cut:
2 strips, 1" x 42"; crosscut into
    5 rectangles, 1" x 9"

From *each of 3* of the green and/or gray prints, cut:
1 rectangle, 3½" x 9" (3 total)

From *each of the remaining 2* green and/or gray prints, cut:
1 rectangle, 3½" x 9" (2 total)
1 rectangle, 2" x 3½" (2 total)

From the white solid, cut:
4 strips, 1½" x 38½"

From the large-scale print, cut:
1 strip, 8½" x 38½"

From the green print for binding, cut:
3 strips, 2½" x 42"

Assembling the Runner

1. Sew a red rectangle to each of the five green and/or gray 3½" x 9" rectangles along the long edges to make a strip set; press. Square up the short end of each strip set and crosscut each one into four segments, 2" wide (20 total).

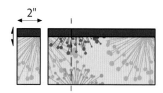

Make 5 strip sets.
Cut 4 segments from each (20 total).

2. Randomly sew 10 segments together along the short edges as shown, making sure the green and gray rectangles alternate with the red rectangles. Sew one of the gray or green 2" x 3½" rectangles to the red rectangle at the end of the strip; press the seam allowances open. Repeat to make a total of two strips.

Make 2.

3. Sew a white strip to each side of the pieced rows; press the seam allowances open.

4. Sew the borders from step 3 to the long edges of the large-scale print strip. Press the seam allowances open.

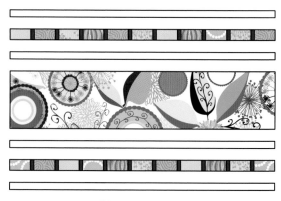

Table-runner assembly

Finishing

Go to ShopMartingale.com/HowtoQuilt if you need more information on any of the finishing steps.

1. Layer, baste, and quilt your table runner.

2. Using the green 2½"-wide strips, prepare and attach the binding.

A Taste of Turquoise

More than a mere "taste," this design serves up a heaping variety of turquoise. Playful pinwheels create a bit of pizzazz, while rich brown prints provide balance. This runner makes a great gift or a treat for your own home.

FINISHED RUNNER: 25½" x 49½" • **FINISHED BLOCK:** 6" x 6"
Designed and made by Heather Willms

Materials

Yardage is based on 42"-wide fabric.

1 yard *total* of assorted turquoise prints for blocks
½ yard *total* of assorted brown prints for blocks
⅜ yard of cream print for block corners and inner border
⅞ yard of brown print for outer border and binding
1¾ yards of fabric for backing
31" x 55" piece of batting

Cutting

From the assorted turquoise prints, cut a *total* of:
72 squares, 3⅞" x 3⅞"

From the assorted brown prints, cut a *total* of:
12 squares, 3⅞" x 3⅞"
24 squares, 2" x 2"

From the cream print, cut:
3 strips, 2" x 42"; cut into
    48 squares, 2" x 2"
4 strips, 1" x 42"

From the brown print for border and binding, cut:
4 strips, 3½" x 42"
4 strips, 2½" x 42"

Making the Blocks

1 Draw a diagonal line from corner to corner on the wrong side of a turquoise 3⅞" square. Layer the marked square on an unmarked turquoise square, right sides together. Sew ¼" from each side of the line. Cut the squares apart on the line and press open to make two half-square-triangle units.

2 Repeat step 1 with all of the turquoise and brown 3⅞" squares to make 72 turquoise units and 12 brown units.

3 Sew four turquoise half-square-triangle units together as shown to create a pinwheel.

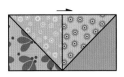

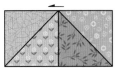

4 Repeat step 3 to make 18 turquoise pinwheels and 3 brown pinwheels.

47

5 Mark the wrong side of each cream and brown 2" square as in step 1. With right sides together, layer a cream square on one corner of a turquoise pinwheel, aligning two sides of the cream square with the outside edges of the pinwheel. Refer to the placement guides below for assistance. Stitch on the marked line. Trim the seam allowances to ¼" and press the resulting cream triangle toward the corner. Repeat on the remaining three corners of the turquoise pinwheel. Make eight blocks with four cream corners, two blocks with four brown corners, and eight blocks with two cream corners and two brown corners. The three brown Pinwheel blocks will remain plain, without 2" squares sewn to them.

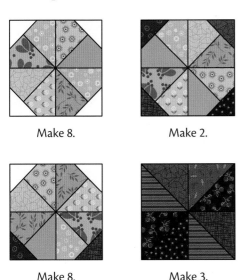

Make 8.   Make 2.

Make 8.   Make 3.

Assembling the Runner

1 Lay out the blocks in rows as shown at right. Sew the blocks in each row together, pressing the seam allowances in opposite directions from row to row. Sew the rows together and press.

2 Sew the cream 1"-wide strips end to end to create one long strip. Measure the length of the runner through the center. Cut two cream strips to fit. Sew them to each long side of the runner. Press seam allowances toward the cream strips.

3 Measure the width of the runner through the center (including the cream borders you added in step 2). Cut two cream strips to fit. Sew them to the short sides of the runner. Press the seam allowances toward the cream strips.

4 Repeat steps 2 and 3 with the brown 3½"-wide strips. Press the seam allowances toward the brown strips.

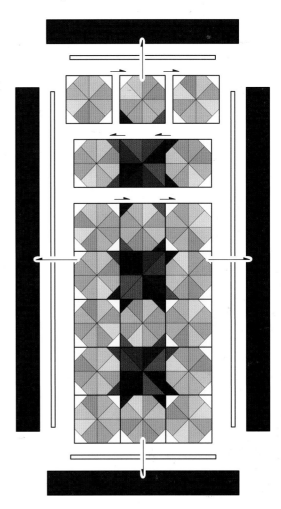

Finishing

Go to ShopMartingale.com/HowtoQuilt if you need more information on any of the finishing steps.

1 Layer, baste, and quilt your table runner.

2 Using the brown-print 2½"-wide strips, prepare and attach the binding.

Farmhouse Favorite

Whether you live in a farmhouse or daydream of doing so, this Log Cabin runner is well suited to the farmhouse style. Use it to grace a long hand-hewn table or display it on a modern one—either way, you'll enjoy making this runner from a selection of fat quarters and showing it off when company comes a-calling.

FINISHED RUNNER: 24½" x 74½" • **FINISHED BLOCK:** 10" x 10"
Designed by Kathy Brown; pieced by Linda Reed; quilted by Carol Hilton

Materials

Yardage is based on 42"-wide fabric. Fat quarters are 18" x 21".

1 fat quarter *each* of blue, red, brown, green, and tan prints for blocks
1⅞ yards of gold solid for blocks, border, and binding
2½ yards of fabric for backing
33" x 83" piece of batting

Cutting

To cut the fat quarters efficiently, lay them all right side up, one on top of the other in a uniform stack. Trim the left and bottom edges of the stack to square them up. Refer to the cutting diagram at right to cut the layered fabrics as indicated.

From the gold solid, cut:
20 strips, 2½" x 42"; crosscut
   8 of the strips into:
      12 squares, 2½" x 2½"
      12 strips, 2½" x 4½"
      12 strips, 2½" x 6½"
      12 strips, 2½" x 8½"
2 squares, 10½" x 10½"

From *each* fat quarter, cut:
6 strips, 2½" x 21"; crosscut into:
   3 squares, 2½" x 2½" (15 total;
     3 will be extra)
   3 strips, 2½" x 4½" (15 total;
     3 will be extra)
   3 strips, 2½" x 6½" (15 total;
     3 will be extra)
   3 strips, 2½" x 8½" (15 total;
     3 will be extra)
   3 strips, 2½" x 10½" (15 total;
     3 will be extra)

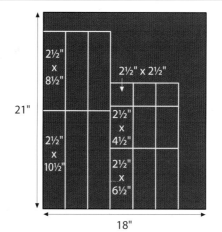

Making the Blocks

This table runner is composed of Log Cabin blocks stitched in five different color combinations to make the best use of your fat quarters. Press the seam allowances as indicated by the arrows in the diagrams.

Block A

Sew a blue 2½" square to the bottom of a gold 4½" strip. Add a gold 6½" strip to the right as shown. Sew a tan 4½" strip to the bottom. Add a gold 8½" strip to the right as shown. Sew a gold 2½" square to the top of a green 6½" strip; sew it to the left side as shown. Sew a brown 8½" strip to the bottom. Sew a red 10½" strip to the left to complete block A. Make two.

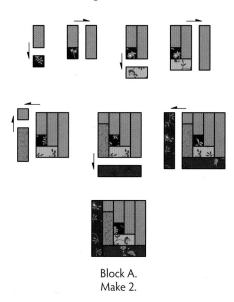

Block A.
Make 2.

Block C

Sew a brown 2½" square to the bottom of a gold 4½" strip. Add a gold 6½" strip to the right as shown. Sew a red 4½" strip to the bottom. Add a gold 8½" strip to the right as shown. Sew a gold 2½" square to the top of a blue 6½" strip; sew it to the left side as shown. Sew a tan 8½" strip to the bottom. Sew a green 10½" strip to the left to complete block C. Make three.

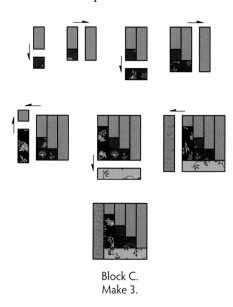

Block C.
Make 3.

Block B

Sew a red 2½" square to the bottom of a gold 4½" strip. Add a gold 6½" strip to the right as shown. Sew a blue 4½" strip to the bottom. Add a gold 8½" strip to the right as shown. Sew a gold 2½" square to the top of a tan 6½" strip; sew it to the left side as shown. Sew a green 8½" strip to the bottom. Sew a brown 10½" strip to the left to complete block B. Make three.

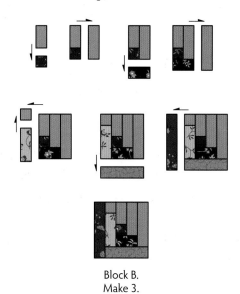

Block B.
Make 3.

Block D

Sew a green 2½" square to the bottom of a gold 4½" strip. Add a gold 6½" strip to the right as shown. Sew a brown 4½" strip to the bottom. Add a gold 8½" strip to the right as shown. Sew a gold 2½" square to the top of a red 6½" strip; sew it to the left side as shown. Sew a blue 8½" strip to the bottom. Sew a tan 10½" strip to the left to complete block D. Make two.

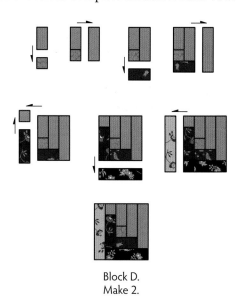

Block D.
Make 2.

Block E

Sew a tan 2½" square to the bottom of a gold 4½" strip. Add a gold 6½" strip to the right as shown. Sew a green 4½" strip to the bottom. Add a gold 8½" strip to the right as shown. Sew a gold 2½" square to the top of a brown 6½" strip; sew it to the left side as shown. Sew a red 8½" strip to the bottom. Sew a blue 10½" strip to the left to complete block E. Make two.

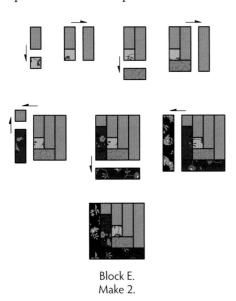

Block E.
Make 2.

Assembling the Runner

1 Using a design wall or other flat surface, arrange the completed blocks and gold 10½" squares into seven rows as shown in the assembly diagram.

2 Sew the blocks into rows, pressing the seam allowances in opposite directions from row to row. Sew the rows together; press the seam allowances in one direction.

3 Sew two gold 2½" x 42" strips together to make one long strip; make two. Stitch the strips to the long sides of the runner top, and then trim the excess even with the ends of the runner. Press the seam allowances toward the border strips. Sew gold 2½" x 42" strips to the short sides of the runner. Trim the excess even with the sides

of the runner top. Press the seam allowances toward the strips.

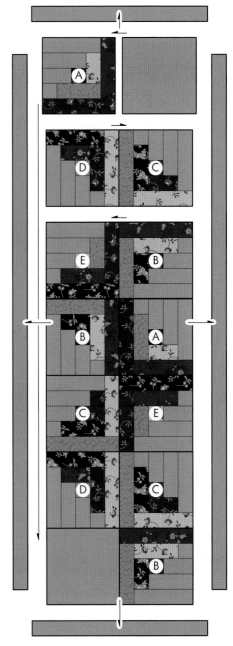

Quilt assembly

Finishing

Go to ShopMartingale.com/HowtoQuilt if you need more information on any of the finishing steps.

1 Layer, baste, and quilt your table runner.

2 Using the remaining six gold 2½"-wide strips, prepare and attach the binding.

Wrapped Up in Ribbons

This whimsical table runner sets the mood for a merry Christmas. The center section consists of three easy blocks, adorned with just a little appliqué. The zigzag border adds some pizzazz and is made from simple flying-geese units. It's easy enough for a confident beginner and would make a great last-minute gift.

FINISHED RUNNER: 16½" x 34½"
FINISHED PACKAGE BLOCK: 8" x 8"
Designed and made by Cheryl Almgren Taylor

Materials
Yardage is based on 42"-wide fabric.

⅞ yard of red polka dot for ribbon appliqués, flying-geese units, and binding
⅓ yard of holly print for block backgrounds and third border
⅓ yard of cream print for sashing, first border, and flying-geese units
⅓ yard of green check for ribbon appliqués and flying-geese units
¼ yard of candy cane print for block background
⅛ yard of red print for blocks and ribbon appliqués
⅛ yard of green print for blocks and ribbon appliqués
⅔ yard of fabric for backing
20" x 38" piece of batting
Fusible web (optional)

Cutting

From the holly print, cut:
1 strip, 4" x 42"; crosscut into
    8 squares, 4" x 4"
3 strips, 1½" x 42"

From the red print, cut:
1 strip, 1½" x 42"; crosscut into:
    2 rectangles, 1½" x 8½"
    4 rectangles, 1½" x 4"

From the candy cane print, cut:
4 squares, 4" x 4"

From the green print, cut:
1 strip, 1½" x 42"; crosscut into:
    1 rectangle, 1½" x 8½"
    2 rectangles, 1½" x 4"

From the cream print, cut:
6 strips, 1½" x 42"; crosscut into:
    2 strips, 1½" x 26½"
    2 rectangles, 1½" x 10½"
    2 rectangles, 1½" x 8½"
    80 squares, 1½" x 1½"

From the red polka dot, cut:
6 strips, 1½" x 42"; crosscut into:
    38 rectangles, 1½" x 2½"
    76 squares, 1½" x 1½"
2 squares, 2⅞" x 2⅞"
2½"-wide bias strips to total
    112" in length

From the green check, cut:
2 strips, 2½" x 42"; crosscut into
    38 rectangles, 1½" x 2½"
2 squares, 2⅞" x 2⅞"

Making the Blocks

1 Sew a red-print 1½" x 4" rectangle between two holly-print 4" squares. Press the seam allowances toward the red rectangle. Repeat to make a total of four units.

Make 4.

2 Sew a red-print 1½" x 8½" rectangle between two units from step 1 to complete the block background. Press the seam allowances toward the red rectangle. Repeat to make a total of two block background squares.

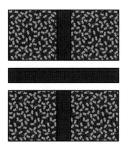

Make 2.

3 Repeat steps 1 and 2 with the candy cane print squares and the green-print rectangles to make one additional block background square.

4 Using the patterns on page 59, prepare the ribbons from the fabrics indicated for your preferred method of appliqué. Cheryl used fusible-web appliqué with machine stitching; for details on appliqué techniques, go to ShopMartingale.com/HowtoQuilt.

5 Refer to the bow placement guide to arrange the prepared red bow appliqué pieces on the holly print block background squares and the green bow appliqué pieces on the candy cane print block background square in the order indicated. Appliqué the shapes in place.

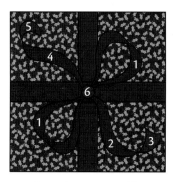

Bow placement guide

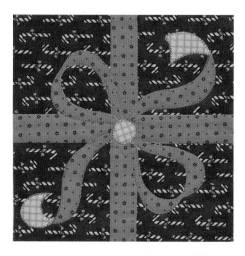

6 If desired, finish the raw edges of each appliqué piece using a blanket stitch, zigzag stitch, or satin stitch.

Assembling the Runner

1 With the candy cane print block in the center, alternately sew the blocks and two cream 1½" x 8½" rectangles together. Be careful to orient the blocks correctly. Press the seam allowances toward the blocks. Add the cream 1½" x 26½" strips to the long edges of the joined blocks. Press the seam allowances toward the blocks. Join the cream 1½" x 10½" rectangles to the short edges of the joined blocks. Press the seam allowances toward the blocks. The table-runner top must

measure 10½" x 28½" for the pieced flying-geese border to fit correctly.

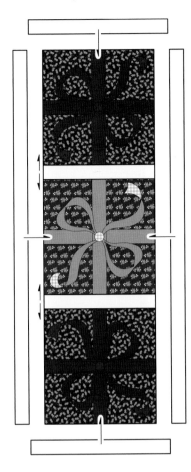

2 To make the flying-geese units for the pieced border, draw a diagonal line from corner to corner on the wrong side of each cream and each red polka dot 1½" square.

3 Position a marked cream square on one end of each red polka dot 1½" x 2½" rectangle, right sides together. Sew on the marked line. Trim ¼" from the stitching. Press the seam allowances toward the red rectangle. Repeat on the opposite end, orienting the marked line as shown. Set aside the four remaining cream squares. Repeat with the red polka dot squares and the green-checked 1½" x 2½" rectangles.

Make 38.   Make 38.

4 Draw a diagonal line from corner to corner on the wrong side of the green checked 2⅞" squares. Lay a marked square on each red polka dot 2⅞" square, right sides together. Sew ¼" from both sides of the marked line. Cut the squares apart on the marked line. Each pair of squares will yield two half-square-triangle units. Press the seam allowances toward the red triangles.

5 Place a marked cream square that you previously set aside on the red corner of each half-square-triangle unit. Sew on the marked lines. Cut ¼" from the stitching. Press the seam allowances toward the red fabric.

Make 4.

6 Sew 14 red-and-cream flying-geese units together side by side, joining them into pairs first. Make sure all the red points are facing the same direction. Repeat to make a total of two rows. Press the seam allowances in one direction. Repeat with the green-and-red flying-geese units, but press the seam allowances in the opposite direction as the red-and-cream units. Join the red-and-cream strip to the top of the green-and-red strip, making sure the red and green points are facing the same direction.

Make 2.

7 Refer to the assembly diagram below to sew the pieced border strips to the long edges of the table-runner top, positioning the cream side of each strip against the cream inner border. Press the seam allowances toward the pieced borders.

8 Repeat step 6 with five red-and-cream and five green-and-red flying-geese units. Make two. Sew a unit from step 5 to each end of each strip so that the same colors butt against each other and the seam allowances match. Join these strips to the short edges of the runner top. Press the seam allowances toward the pieced borders.

9 Sew the holly-print 1½"-wide strips end to end to create one long strip. Measure the length of the runner through the center. Cut two holly print strips to fit, and sew them to the long sides of the runner. Press the seam allowances toward the holly print border.

10 Measure the width of the runner through the center (including the borders just added). Cut two holly-print strips to fit, and sew them to the short sides of the runner. Press the seam allowances toward the holly-print border.

Finishing

Go to ShopMartingale.com/HowtoQuilt if you need more information on any of the finishing steps.

1 Layer, baste, and quilt your table runner.

2 Using the red polka dot 2½"-wide strips, prepare and attach the bias binding.

Quilt assembly

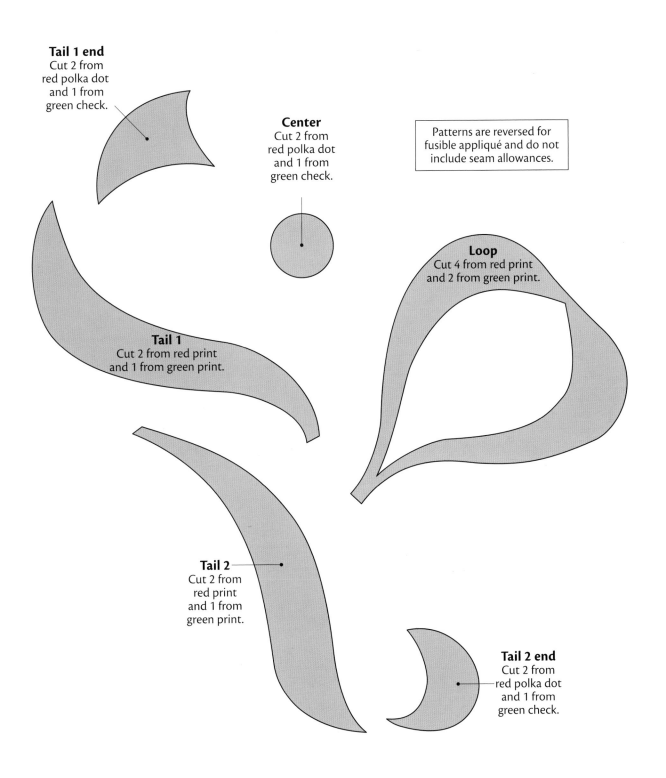

Tail 1 end
Cut 2 from red polka dot and 1 from green check.

Center
Cut 2 from red polka dot and 1 from green check.

Patterns are reversed for fusible appliqué and do not include seam allowances.

Loop
Cut 4 from red print and 2 from green print.

Tail 1
Cut 2 from red print and 1 from green print.

Tail 2
Cut 2 from red print and 1 from green print.

Tail 2 end
Cut 2 from red polka dot and 1 from green check.

Pie Birds

Gather together strips and scraps of your favorite prints, and then weave some magic as you piece this table runner featuring a graceful gaggle of patchwork geese.

FINISHED RUNNER: 14⅝" x 43" • **FINISHED BLOCK:** 10" x 10"
Designed and made by Kim Diehl; quilted by Deborah Poole

Materials

Yardage is based on 42"-wide fabric.

1¼ yards *total* of assorted print scraps, ranging from 2" to 6" in length, for blocks

⅞ yard of black print for blocks and binding

1 yard of fabric for backing

21" x 49" piece of batting

Cutting

From the assorted print scraps, cut a *total* of:

7 squares, 2½" x 2½"

14 squares, 1⅞" x 1⅞"; cut each square in half diagonally to yield 28 triangles

56 rectangles, 1½" x 2½"

56 rectangles, 1½" x 3½"

56 rectangles, 1½" x 4½"

28 rectangles, 1½" x 5½"

From the black print, cut:

1 strip, 1⅞" x 42"; crosscut into 14 squares, 1⅞" x 1⅞". Cut each square in half diagonally to yield 28 triangles.

9 strips, 1½" x 42"; crosscut into 196 squares, 1½" x 1½"

4 strips, 2½" x 42"

Making the Blocks

1 Layer a print and a black 1⅞" triangle, right sides together. Stitch the pair together along the long diagonal edges. Press the seam allowances toward the black triangles. Trim away the dog-ear points. Repeat for a total of 28 half-square-triangle units.

Make 28.

2 Using a pencil and an acrylic ruler, draw a diagonal line on the wrong side of each black 1½" square.

3 Layer a prepared black square on one end of a print 1½" x 2½" rectangle, right sides together. Sew on the marked line. Trim the excess fabric ¼" from the stitching line. Press the seam allowances toward the black print. Repeat for a total of 28 pieced rectangle units measuring 1½" x 2½" and 28 mirror-image 1½" x 2½" rectangle units.

Make 28 of each.

4 Repeat step 3 with the remaining black squares and assorted-print rectangles to make:
- 28 pieced 1½" x 3½" rectangle units and 28 pieced 1½" x 3½" mirror-image rectangle units
- 28 pieced 1½" x 4½" rectangle units and 28 pieced 1½" x 4½" mirror-image rectangle units
- 14 pieced 1½" x 5½" rectangle units and 14 pieced 1½" x 5½" mirror-image rectangle units

5 Join two half-square-triangle units from step 1 as shown. Press the seam allowances open. Repeat for a total of 14 block rows measuring 1½" x 2½".

Make 14.

6 Join a pieced 1½" x 2½" rectangle unit and a pieced 1½" x 2½" mirror-image rectangle unit as shown. Press the seam allowances open. Repeat for a total of 28 block rows measuring 4½" long.

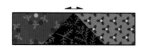

Make 28.

7 Repeat step 6 using one pieced rectangle and one mirror-image pieced rectangle of the same length to make:
- 28 block rows measuring 1½" x 6½"
- 28 block rows measuring 1½" x 8½"
- 14 block rows measuring 1½" x 10½"

8 Join pieced 2½"-long block rows to opposite sides of an assorted-print 2½" square. Press the seam allowances toward the print square. Join pieced 4½"-long block rows to the top and bottom edges. Press the seam allowances toward the just-added rows.

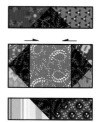
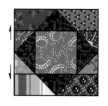

9 Join pieced 4½"-long block rows to opposite sides of the unit from step 8. Press the seam allowances toward the just-added rows. Join pieced 6½"-long block rows to the top and bottom edges. Press the seam allowances toward the just-added rows.

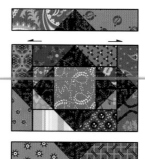
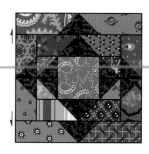

10 Continue building and stitching the patchwork unit in the same manner, using the remaining sizes of pieced block rows from the shortest to longest lengths. The finished block should measure 10½" square, including seam allowances.

11 Repeat steps 8–10 to make a total of seven pieced blocks.

Make 7.

Assembling the Runner

1 Lay out the blocks in three rows as shown. Join the blocks in each horizontal row. Press the seam allowances open. Join the rows, beginning and ending with two or three backstitches to secure the seam ends. Press the seam allowances away from the middle row.

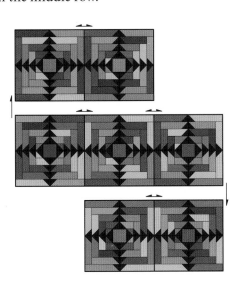

2 Place the pieced rows on point. To trim the sides of the runner, be sure to measure *out* ¼" from the seam intersection of the center squares, use a rotary cutter and an acrylic ruler to trim away the excess portion of the side blocks.

Trim.

Finishing

Go to ShopMartingale.com/HowtoQuilt if you need more information on any of the finishing steps.

1 Layer, baste, and quilt your table runner.

2 Using the black-print 2½"-wide strips, prepare and attach the binding.

Star Spangled

Choose a pack of your favorite 5" charm squares or delve into your stash for this cute-as-can-be star quilt. Mix together reds and blues for a patriotic feel, or make it fun and scrappy for more of a farmhouse style. Whatever fabrics you use, it's guaranteed to delight.

FINISHED RUNNER: 12" x 30" • **FINISHED BLOCK:** 6" x 6"
Designed and made by Mary Etherington and Connie Tesene

Materials

Yardage is based on 42"-wide fabric. Charm squares are 5" x 5".

40 charm squares of assorted prints for patchwork, divided roughly as follows: 12 bright red, 10 light, 10 colonial blue, and 8 medium brown
¼ yard of red fabric for binding
⅝ yard of fabric for backing
18" x 36" piece of batting

● MAKING DO

If you don't have a set of precut charm squares, you'll need one fat eighth (9" x 21") *each* of six assorted red prints, five assorted light prints, five assorted blue prints, and four assorted brown prints. Cut four squares, 2" x 2", and four squares, 2⅜" x 2⅜", from each fabric.

Cutting

From *each* charm square, cut:
2 squares, 2⅜" x 2⅜" (80 total)*
2 squares, 2" x 2" (80 total)*

From the red binding fabric, cut:
3 strips, 2¼" x 42"

*Keep squares of the same fabric together.

Making the Blocks

Each block is made from two pairs of fabrics.

1. Pair 2⅜" squares into darks and lights or accents and backgrounds, keeping the same fabrics together. In the quilt shown, a bright red square was generally paired with a brown square, while a blue square was paired with a light square. You need to pair each fabric with one that contrasts with it.

2 Place a pair of charm squares from step 1 right sides together. Draw a diagonal line from corner to corner on the wrong side of the lighter square. Stitch ¼" from each side of the line. Cut apart on the line and press the seam allowances toward the darker triangles. Repeat with the remaining pairs of 2⅜" squares to make 20 sets with four matching half-square-triangle units in each set.

Make 20 sets of 4 matching triangle units (80 total).

3 Arrange two matching half-square-triangle units with two matching 2" squares, being careful to orient them as shown. Sew the triangles and squares together, pressing the seam allowances toward the squares. Sew these units together and press seam allowances open. Repeat to make two identical units for each block (20 pairs total).

Make 20 matching pairs.

4 Pair two matching red/brown units from step 3 with two matching blue/light units. Arrange and sew together as shown. Press the seam allowances open to help the blocks lie flat when sewn together. Repeat to make 10 blocks.

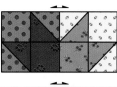
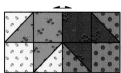
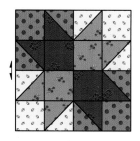

Make 10.

Assembling the Runner

Sew the blocks together into five rows of two blocks each. Press the seam allowances open. Join the rows; press.

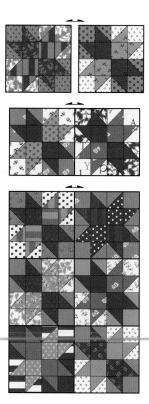

Finishing

Go to ShopMartingale.com/HowtoQuilt if you need more information on any of the finishing steps.

1 Layer, baste, and quilt your table runner.

2 Using the red 2¼"-wide strips, prepare and attach the binding.

Window Panes

Connie and Mary, retired owners of the former Country Threads quilt shop, say, "In our sample a couple of blocks have the lighter fabric of a half-square-triangle unit facing the blue square. Would you notice if we hadn't mentioned it? An occasional deviation from the pattern adds a bit of interest, much like taking a side trip on a back road instead of staying on the interstate."

FINISHED RUNNER: 20" x 48½" • **FINISHED BLOCK:** 8½" x 8½"
Designed and made by Mary Etherington and Connie Tesene

Materials

Yardage is based on 42"-wide fabric. Charm squares are 5" x 5"; a fat eighth is 9" x 21".

40 charm squares, divided fairly evenly between light and dark values for blocks
⅔ yard of brown tone on tone for wide sashing and border
⅛ yard *each* of 2 brown prints for narrow sashing in blocks
1 fat eighth of blue print for cornerstones
⅓ yard of red print for binding
1¾ yards of fabric for backing
26" x 55" piece of batting

Cutting

From *each* of the 2 brown prints, cut:
20 rectangles, 1" x 4½" (40 total)

From the blue print, cut:
10 squares, 1" x 1"

From the brown tone on tone, cut:
8 strips, 1½" x 42"; crosscut 5 of the strips into:
5 rectangles, 1½" x 9"
6 strips, 1½" x 18½"

From the red print, cut:
4 strips, 2¼" x 42"

⬤ MAKING DO

If you don't have a set of precut charm squares, you'll need one fat quarter (18" x 21") *each* of four red, four tan or off-white, and three medium to dark taupe fabrics.

Making the Blocks

1. Pair the 20 light charm squares with the 20 dark charm squares, right sides together, and draw a diagonal line from corner to corner on the wrong side of the light squares.

2. Stitch ¼" from each side of the line. Cut in half along the line, creating two matching half-square-triangle units. Press the seam allowances toward the darker fabric. Trim the units to measure 4½" x 4½". Repeat to make 40 half-square-triangle units.

3. Arrange four assorted half-square-triangle units, four brown 1" x 4½" rectangles, and one blue 1" square as shown, being careful to orient the darker triangles toward the blue square. Sew the units together to make a block. Press the seam allowances toward the brown rectangles. Repeat to make 10 blocks.

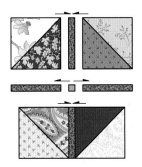 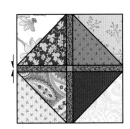

Make 10.

Assembling the Runner

1. Sew together two blocks with a brown 1½" x 9" sashing rectangle in between. Repeat to make five rows of two blocks each. Sew the rows together, adding a brown 1½" x 18½" sashing strip between each row and at each end of the runner top. Press the seam allowances toward the sashing.

2. Sew the three brown 1½" x 42" strips together end to end to make a long strip. Press the seam allowances open. From this long strip, cut two borders, 1½" x 49". Sew the borders to the long sides of the runner top. Press the seam allowances toward the borders.

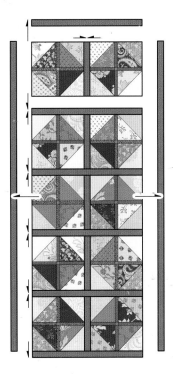

Finishing

Go to ShopMartingale.com/HowtoQuilt if you need more information on any of the finishing steps.

1. Layer, baste, and quilt your table runner.

2. Using the red 2¼"-wide strips, prepare and attach the binding.

Pink Posies

Isn't there something special about a collection of antique buttons? Here, an assortment of simple white buttons embellish this table runner. Felted wool and a touch of rickrack add to the homey, vintage charm.

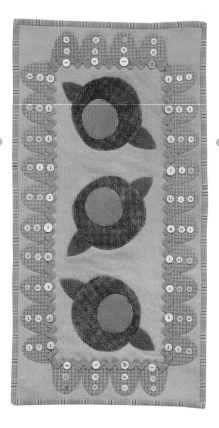

FINISHED RUNNER: 13" x 25"
Designed and made by Avis Shirer

Materials

Cotton yardage is based on 42"-wide fabric. All wool is presumed to be felted wool, which is wool that has been washed and dried by machine to shrink the fibers and prevent raveling. If you are purchasing unfelted wool off the bolt, purchase extra to allow for shrinkage. To felt wool, machine wash in warm water and dry on a medium setting.

Wool

13" x 25" rectangle of off-white for foundation

10" x 25" rectangle of off-white houndstooth checked for tongues

6" x 18" rectangle of rose for outer flowers

4" x 12" rectangle of soft pink for flower centers

2" x 12" rectangle of green for leaves

Cotton

¼ yard of tan stripe for binding
½ yard of fabric for backing

Additional Materials

2 yards of tan medium rickrack
Fusible web
84 assorted off-white and white buttons, ¼" to ⅝" diameter
Chalk marker

Cutting

The appliqué patterns for the flowers and leaves are on page 73. Prepare the shapes for your preferred method of appliqué from the fabrics indicated. Avis used fusible-web appliqué with machine stitching; for details on appliqué techniques, go to ShopMartingale.com/HowtoQuilt.

From the rose wool, cut:
3 outer flowers

From the pink wool, cut:
3 flower centers

From the green wool, cut:
6 leaves

From the tan cotton, cut:
2 strips, 1½" x 42"

Assembling the Runner

1. Make sure that the off-white foundation piece measures 13" x 25". Using a chalk marker, draw a line 2½" in from the outer edges.

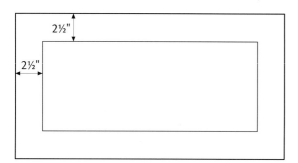

2. Trace the tongue pattern on page 73 onto the paper side of the fusible web. When tracing, do not make individual tongues, but rather trace in one continuous strip. For the ends, trace two units with 4 tongues each; for the sides, trace two units with 10 tongues each. Roughly cut around the units.

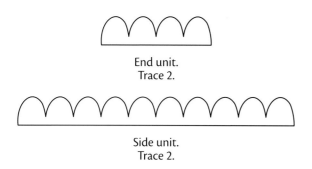

End unit.
Trace 2.

Side unit.
Trace 2.

3. Following the manufacturer's instructions, fuse the tongue units to the wrong side of the off-white houndstooth wool piece and cut them out. Position the tongue units on the foundation piece, aligning the straight edges with the drawn lines; fuse them in place. Stitch around each tongue with a blanket stitch and matching thread.

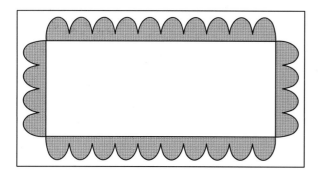

4. Cut two pieces of rickrack 22" long and two pieces 10" long. Turn under 1" on the ends of each piece. Pin the long pieces of rickrack in place along the long straight edges of each tongue side unit, and then pin the short rickrack pieces to the ends. The rickrack can be attached one of two ways: with a machine straight stitch down the center of the rickrack, or by sewing on the inner row of buttons (see step 5) and attaching the rickrack in the process. The latter method will leave the rickrack loose between the buttons, as was done in the featured quilt.

5. Referring to the photo on page 70 for placement, sew on the buttons. Align the inner row of buttons on top of the rickrack so they are centered on the long edge of the tongues. Sew two additional buttons to each tongue, aligning them with the first button.

6. Position the outer flowers on the table-runner top. Place a flower center on each outer flower, and then tuck the straight edge of two leaves under each outer flower. When you are happy with the placement, appliqué the shapes in place. If desired, machine blanket stitch around each appliqué with matching thread.

Finishing

Go to ShopMartingale.com/HowtoQuilt if you need more information on any of the finishing steps.

1. Baste the table-runner top to the backing and quilt as desired.

2. Using the striped 1½"-wide strips, prepare and attach the binding. (Avis used single-fold binding, not double-fold.)

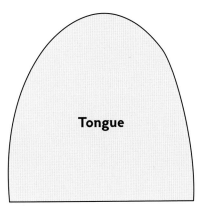

Tongue

Patterns do not include
seam allowances.

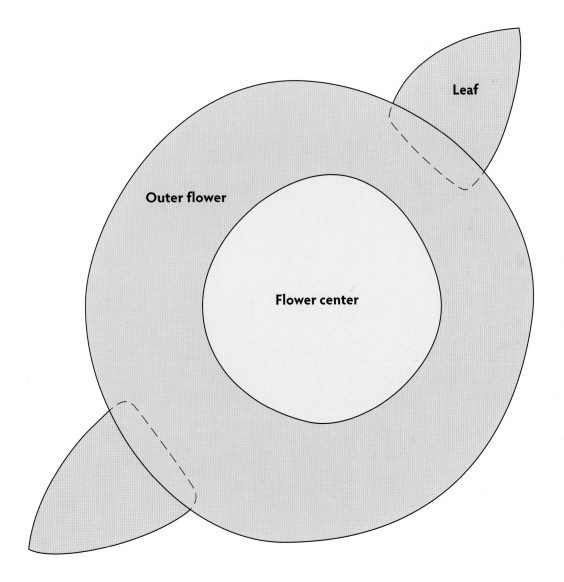

Leaf

Outer flower

Flower center

Poinsettias

Who would guess that this Christmas table runner is as quick and easy to make as it is elegant? You can stitch one up in no time for a lovely hostess present or for anyone on your holiday gift list. The secret is starting with silk flowers from the craft department!

FINISHED RUNNER: 17½" x 41"

Designed and made by Karen Costello Soltys

Materials

Yardage is based on 42"-wide fabric.

1 yard of light green print for table runner and backing

2¼ yards of ⅜"-wide red ribbon*

20" x 44" piece of low-loft batting or fusible fleece

2¼ yards of ⅜"-wide fusible web, such as HeatnBond or Stitch Witchery

½ yard of 20"-wide fusible web

4 silk poinsettia blossoms

Gold heat-set crystals, seed beads, or buttons for poinsettia centers

Parchment paper

*Karen used a glitter ribbon, but grosgrain or velvet ribbons work well, too.

Quilting the Runner

1 Cut the light green print in half crosswise to make two pieces, approximately 18" x 42". Remove the selvages and layer the fabric pieces, right sides together, on top of the batting. If you're using fusible fleece, fuse it to the wrong side of one of the green fabric pieces, and then layer the other piece on top. Pin the layers together around the perimeter.

2 Starting on one short end about 1" from a corner, sew around the perimeter of the layers using a ¼" seam allowance and stopping after you sew about 1" past the last corner. Leave the rest of this short end open for turning. A walking foot is helpful for this step if you have one.

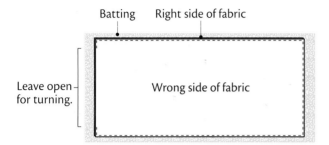

Batting   Right side of fabric

Leave open for turning.   Wrong side of fabric

3 Trim the excess batting and clip the corners. Turn the table runner right side out and press flat, turning in the raw edges at the open end. Topstitch ¼" from the edge all around the table runner to ensure the edges won't roll. Then edgestitch around the runner. This will secure the open end.

4 Quilt the center of the table runner as desired. Karen quilted the one shown in an allover meander pattern.

Embellishing the Runner

1 Cut four lengths of ribbon about 19" long. Peel the paper off one side of the ⅜"-wide fusible web and position the adhesive side down on the wrong side of the ribbon. Fuse in place. (If you're using Stitch Witchery that doesn't have paper, place parchment paper over the ribbon and fusible product so that it won't adhere to your iron.)

2 Using a rotary-cutting ruler as a guide, measure 3" from one short end of the table runner and align one length of ribbon against the ruler. Remove the ruler and fuse in place, folding the ribbon under at each end so that the ends align with the edges of the table runner. These ends will be stitched in place later. Position a second ribbon 1½" from the first and fuse in the same manner. Machine stitch close to the ribbon edges using matching thread to secure.

3 Repeat step 2 to add ribbon to the other end of the table runner.

4 To make the poinsettia appliqués, peel the silk flower petals from the plastic stems, peeling from the stem end out toward the end of the petal. At the ironing board, position the petals on the adhesive side of the fusible web, grouping the petals for each flower so that you can keep them organized.

5 Place the parchment paper over the top to protect your iron from the exposed adhesive. (If you're using Steam-A-Seam, you won't need parchment, as it has paper on both sides. Simply peel the paper off one side, position the petals right side up, and then replace the paper layer over the top.) Fuse, referring to the manufacturer's instructions and taking care not to scorch the petals.

● FUSE LIGHTLY!

To prevent scorching, fuse for just a second or two from the top, then carefully flip all of the petal and paper layers over and fuse again from the back. That's the side where the adhesive is, which means it adheres more quickly to the petals this way. And you won't have to use a hot iron for too long on the delicate petals.

6 Once the fusible web has cooled, cut out around the perimeter of each petal. If any of the petals have frayed a bit, simply trim off the frayed edges. Working with the petals for one flower at a time, peel the paper backing from the petals and position the petals onto the table runner, referring to the photo on page 74 for placement. When satisfied, fuse in place. You may want to use a scrap of fabric as a press cloth to protect the silk petals from the hot iron.

7 Repeat step 6 for each additional flower. You can overlap them for a more natural arrangement, or place them however you like.

8 When all of the flowers are fused in place, add the heat-set crystals for the stamens, or hand stitch seed beads in the flower centers. Another option is to sew yellow or gold buttons in the flower centers.

Bee-U-tiful

If you've never incorporated linen into a quilting project, here's a perfect opportunity. Pat used it for both the background and backing of this lovely table runner. It may not be obvious, but the pieced top is appliquéd to the linen background. This runner creates a warm welcome in any home, and is sized so that it may span the entire length of a dining table with a generous drop on the ends.

FINISHED RUNNER: 21½" x 106½" • **FINISHED BLOCK:** 10" x 10"
Designed by Pat Wys; pieced by Sarah Gafnea; quilted by Leisa Wiggley

Materials

Yardage is based on 42"-wide fabric.

2 yards *total* of 2 or 3 light neutral linens with a small-scale checked pattern for table-runner background

1½ yards *total* of assorted medium and dark neutral prints for blocks, appliqués, and setting units

½ yard of light print for blocks

½ yard *total* of assorted light and medium neutral prints for blocks and setting units

¾ yard of dark print for binding

2½ yards of fabric for backing

27" x 112" piece of batting

Freezer paper (optional)

Cutting

From the assorted light and medium prints, cut:
28 squares, 2½" x 2½"
28 rectangles, 2½" x 6½"

From the light print, cut:
5 strips, 2½" x 42"; crosscut into 28 rectangles, 2½" x 6½"

From the assorted medium and dark prints, cut:
195 squares, 2½" x 2½"

From the neutral linens, cut a *total* of:
3 pieces, 21½" x 36"

From the dark print, cut:
2½"-wide bias strips to total 270" in length

Making the Blocks

1 Lay out nine assorted medium and dark 2½"
squares in a nine-patch formation. When you're
pleased with the arrangement, sew the squares
together in three rows to form the nine-patch
units. Press as indicated. Sew the rows together.
Make seven blocks.

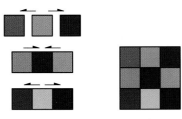

Make 7.

2 Sew light 2½" x 6½" rectangles to the left and
right sides of each nine-patch unit. Press the
seam allowances toward the nine-patch units.

3 Sew a light or medium 2½" square to each
end of the remaining light 2½" x 6½" rectangles.
Press the seam allowances toward the squares.
Make 14.

Make 14.

4 Sew the units from step 3 to the units from
step 2 to complete the blocks. Press the seam
allowances toward the pieced rectangles.
Make seven.

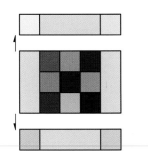

Make 7.

5 Using the appliqué pattern on page 81 and
the assorted medium and dark prints, cut and
prepare 84 teardrop shapes for your favorite
appliqué method. Pat used freezer paper and
mixed some wool shapes in with the cotton.

6 Appliqué three teardrops in each corner to
complete the Honeybee blocks.

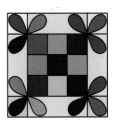

Make 7.

Making the Setting Units

1 Sew a medium or dark 2½" square to each
end of a light or medium 2½" x 6½" rectangle.
Choose squares that are darker than the
rectangles. Press the seam allowances toward
the squares. Make 16.

Make 16.

2 Sew six assorted medium or dark 2½" squares
together as shown. Sew a light or medium
2½" x 6½" rectangle to the long side of the 2½"
squares. Press as indicated. Make 12.

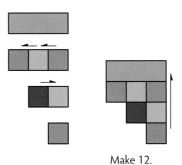

Make 12.

3 Sew a medium or dark 2½" square to one end of the rectangle in the step 2 unit as shown. Press the seam allowances toward the square. Sew a step 1 unit to the side to complete the side setting unit. Press. Make 12.

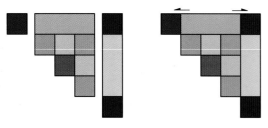

Make 12.

4 Sew four squares together as shown and add a unit from step 1 to make a corner setting unit. Press as indicated. Make four.

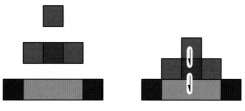

Make 4.

Assembling the Runner

1 Sew side setting units to the left and right sides of five Honeybee blocks as shown. Press the seam allowances toward the setting units.

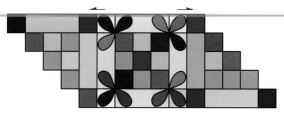

Make 5.

2 Sew a side setting unit to each of the two remaining Honeybee blocks. Press.

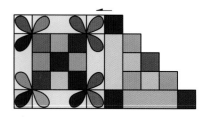

3 Sew the block/setting units together to create the center of the runner. Sew two corner setting units to each end of the runner.

4 Join the three 21½" x 36" linen pieces to make a background measuring 21½" x 107".

5 Layer the table-runner center on the linen background. Lightly spray baste it in place, or add appliqué pins to stabilize it while stitching. Appliqué the runner to the background by hand or machine.

Finishing

1 Pat made the backing from linen. Before appliquéing the pieced portion to the backing, she had the linen layers machine quilted with a free-motion design.

2 After quilting, Pat machine appliquéd the center of the table runner onto the quilted base by turning the edges under, pressing them, and adding a bit of fabric glue to hold them in place. Using monofilament, she added machine quilting in the ditch around all the squares and blocks. This firmly attached the pieced and appliquéd portion to the background quilt.

3 Before binding, cut the corners at an angle to add visual interest.

4 Using the dark print 2½"-wide strips, prepare and attach the bias binding.

Trim corners after quilting.

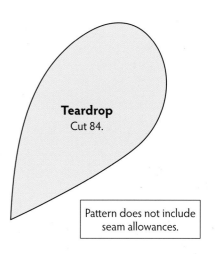

Teardrop
Cut 84.

Pattern does not include seam allowances.

Cottage Garden

Like pennies in a sparkling fountain, colorful appliqué circles seem to cast off little ripples of happiness as they land on this cozy and inviting patchwork table runner. Make a wish, and then scatter some pennies of your own.

FINISHED RUNNER: 12½" x 46½" • **FINISHED BLOCK:** 10" x 10"
Designed and made by Kim Diehl

Materials

Yardage is based on 42"-wide fabric. Fat eighths are 9" x 21".

⅞ yard *total* of assorted light prints for blocks and sashing strips

¾ yard *total* of assorted print scraps (some 6" x 6" and smaller, some 2½"-wide random-length strips) for penny appliqués and binding

1 fat eighth of light brown print for blocks and setting squares

1 fat eighth of green print for stem and leaf appliqués

Assorted scraps of green prints for leaf appliqués

1 yard of fabric for backing

18" x 52" piece of batting

Fusible web (optional)

⅜" bias bar

#8 or #12 pearl cotton

Size 5 embroidery needle

Cutting

Appliqué patterns A–F are on page 86. Kim uses freezer-paper appliqué and machine stitching, but you can prepare the shapes for your favorite method. For more details on appliqué, go to ShopMartingale.com/HowtoQuilt for free information, or see Kim's book Simple Appliqué *(Martingale, 2015) for a variety of appliqué techniques.*

From the assorted light prints, cut a *total* of:

3 squares, 4½" x 4½"
12 rectangles, 1½" x 4½"
12 rectangles, 1½" x 6½"
12 rectangles, 1½" x 8½"
10 rectangles, 1½" x 10½"
12 rectangles, 1½" x 12½"

From the light brown print, cut:

44 squares, 1½" x 1½"

Continued on page 84

Continued from page 82

From the green print fat eighth, cut *on the bias:*
12 rectangles, 1¼" x 5½"
2 rectangles, 1¼" x 8"

From the remainder of the green print, cut:
6 using pattern F

From the assorted print scraps, cut a *total* **of:**
3 each using patterns A, B, C, and D
17 using pattern E
Enough 2½"-wide random lengths to make a 104"
   length of binding when joined end to end

From the assorted green scraps, cut a *total* **of:**
36 using pattern F

Making the Blocks

1 Sew the light 1½" x 4½" rectangles to opposite sides of each light 4½" square. Press the seam allowances toward the rectangles.

Make 3.

2 Join a brown 1½" square to each end of the remaining light 1½" x 4½" rectangles. Sew the resulting pieced rectangles to the remaining sides of the 4½" squares from step 1. Press the seam allowances toward the pieced rectangles.

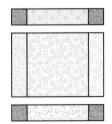

3 Repeat steps 1 and 2 to add the light 1½" x 6½" rectangles, and then the light 1½" x 8½" rectangles to the previous unit to complete the blocks.

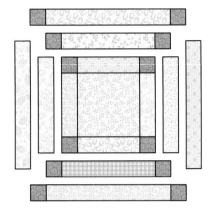

Make 3.

Assembling the Runner

1 Referring to the assembly diagram below, lay out the three pieced blocks in alternating positions with four assorted light 1½" x 10½" rectangles. Join the pieces. Press the seam allowances away from the pieced blocks.

2 Lay out three assorted light 1½" x 10½" rectangles in alternating positions with four brown 1½" squares. Join the pieces. Press the seam allowances toward the rectangles. Repeat for a total of two pieced sashing rows. Join these rows to the long sides of the table runner. Press the seam allowances toward the sashing rows.

3 Join six assorted light 1½" x 12½" rectangles to make a pieced unit. Press the seam allowances in one direction. Repeat for a total of two pieced units. Join these units to the short sides of the table runner. Press the seam allowances away from the table-runner center. The top should now measure 12½" x 46½", including the seam allowances.

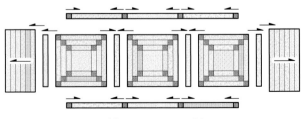

Table-runner assembly

4 Fold each narrow end of the table-runner top in half and finger-press a crease at the center position. Use an acrylic ruler and pencil to draw a diagonal line from each outermost brown square to the creased outer edge of the table runner. (The fabric outside these marked points will be trimmed away after the appliqué is completed.)

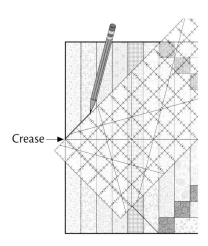

Crease →

5 With wrong sides together, fold each green 1¼"-wide bias rectangle in half lengthwise and use a scant ¼" seam allowance to stitch along the long raw edges to form a tube. Slide the bias bar through each tube to easily press it flat, centering the seam allowance so that it will be hidden from the front of the finished seam. (If the seam allowance will be visible, trim it to ⅛".)

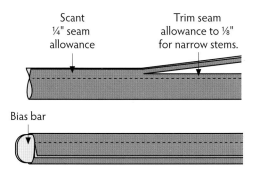

Scant ¼" seam allowance

Trim seam allowance to ⅛" for narrow stems.

Bias bar

6 Place small dots of liquid fabric glue along the seamline underneath the pressed seam allowance at approximately ½" to 1" intervals. Use a hot, dry iron on the wrong side of the stem to heat-set the glue and fuse the seam allowances in place.

7 Center a prepared A penny appliqué over the center square of each pieced block; pin in place. Using the photo on page 82 as a guide, lay out and baste four prepared 5½"-long stems on each block, tucking the raw ends under the A circles approximately ¼". In the same manner, position and baste a prepared 8"-long stem on each outer block, ensuring the stems lie well within the marked triangular areas. Lay out and baste the leaves, positioning them as shown in the photo. Remove the A appliqués.

8 Appliqué the basted stems and leaves in place.

9 Working from the bottom layer to the top, appliqué the A, B, C, D, and E penny appliqués in place on each block, and attach an E circle at the end of each stem.

Finishing

Go to ShopMartingale.com/HowtoQuilt if you need more information on any of the finishing steps.

1 Trim away the excess background fabric exactly on the drawn lines at the ends of the table runner.

2 Layer, baste, and quilt your table runner.

3 Join the assorted 2½"-wide random lengths into a 104"-long strip and use it to bind the runner.

Patterns do not
include seam allowances.

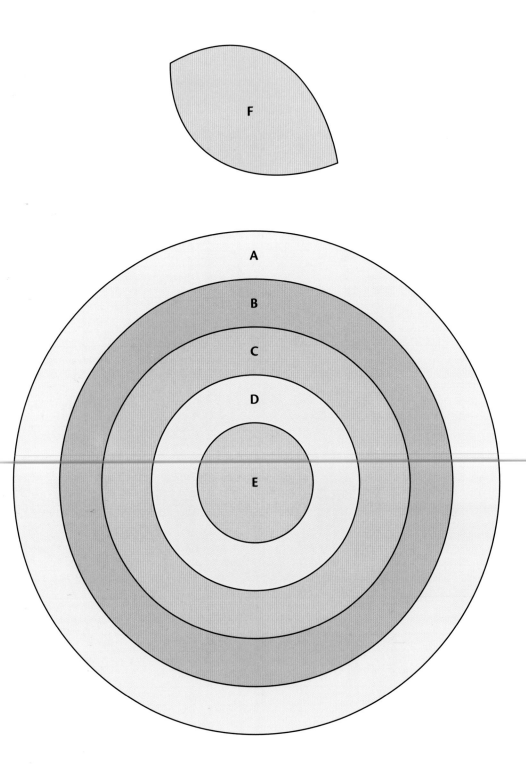

F

A

B

C

D

E

Flying in Formation

Sometimes all the decoration you need is a narrow table runner to dress up the setting. Here, large flying geese all point toward the center of the runner. This runner is so quick and easy that you'll be inclined to make more than one!

FINISHED RUNNER: 8¼" x 57¾" • **FINISHED BLOCK:** 4⅛" x 8¼"

Designed and made by Mary Etherington and Connie Tesene

Materials

Yardage is based on 42"-wide fabric. Charm squares are 5" x 5".

8 charm squares of assorted dark red prints for blocks

6 charm squares of assorted dark green prints for blocks

14 charm squares of assorted tan or cream prints for blocks

½ yard of dark red fabric for binding

⅞ yard of fabric for backing

12" x 60" piece of batting

Cutting

From the dark red fabric for binding, cut:

4 strips, 2¼" x 42"

● MAKING DO

If you don't have a set of precut charm squares, you'll need ¼ yard of a dark red print, ¼ yard of a dark green print, and ⅓ yard of a tan or cream print. Cut your own 5" x 5" squares from these fabrics.

Making the Blocks

1. Draw a diagonal line from corner to corner on the wrong side of the tan or cream squares. Place a marked square on each red charm square, right sides together. Repeat with the green charm squares and the remaining marked tan or cream squares.

2. Stitch ¼" from each side of the line. Cut in half along the line, creating two matching half-square-triangle units. Press the seam allowances toward the darker fabric. Make eight pairs of red-and-cream half-square-triangle units and six pairs of green-and-cream half-square-triangle units (28 total).

Make 16 red.

Make 12 green.

3. Sew two matching half-square-triangle units together as shown to make a Flying Geese block. Press the seam allowances open. Make eight red blocks and six green blocks.

Make 8 red.

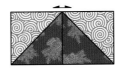
Make 6 green.

Assembling the Runner

Sew the Flying Geese blocks together, alternating red and green blocks and rotating them so the points face the center as shown. Press.

Finishing

Go to ShopMartingale.com/HowtoQuilt if you need more information on any of the finishing steps.

1. Layer, baste, and quilt your table runner.

2. Using the red 2¼"-wide strips, prepare and attach the binding.

Merry, Merry

Let your holiday spirit loose with the rich, warm colors of the season. When outdoor temperatures start to drop, make this table runner and your home will be feeling bright and festive in no time.

FINISHED RUNNER: 18½" x 38½"
Designed and made by Shelley Wicks and Jeanne Large; quilted by Jeanne Large

Materials

Yardage is based on 42"-wide fabric. A fat eighth is 9" x 21".

½ yard of black print for inner border and binding

⅓ yard of red print for outer border

¼ yard *each* of 4 assorted gold prints for background*

1 fat eighth of black print for letters

9" x 12" piece of light gold print for stars

8" x 12" piece of green print for holly leaves

4" x 4" piece of red print for berries

1⅓ yards of fabric for backing

26" x 46" piece of batting

1⅛ yards of ½"-wide green rickrack

Fusible web (optional)

*Number the gold prints from #1 to #4. Gold print #4 will be the background for the appliquéd letters.

Cutting

From gold print #1, cut:
1 strip, 4½" x 42"; crosscut into:
  2 squares, 4½" x 4½"
  2 rectangles, 4½" x 8½"

From gold print #2, cut:
1 strip, 4½" x 42"; crosscut into:
  1 square, 4½" x 4½"
  2 rectangles, 4½" x 8½"

From gold print #3, cut:
1 strip, 4½" x 42"; crosscut into:
  1 square, 4½" x 4½"
  2 rectangles, 4½" x 8½"

From gold print #4, cut:
1 strip, 4½" x 42"; crosscut into 2 rectangles, 4½" x 16½"

From the black print for border and binding, cut:
3 strips, 1½" x 42"; crosscut into:
  2 strips, 1½" x 14½"
  2 strips, 1½" x 32½"
3 strips, 2½" x 42"

From the red print for border, cut:
3 strips, 2½" x 42"; crosscut into:
  2 strips, 2½" x 18½"
  2 strips, 2½" x 34½"

Assembling the Runner

1 Lay out the gold squares and rectangles as shown. Sew them together into rows. Press the seam allowances in opposite directions from row to row. Sew the rows together. Press the seam allowances in one direction.

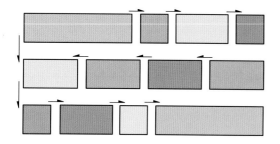

2 Position the green rickrack on the pieced background, shaping it into a gentle curve. Pin in place, trim the excess, and sew down the center of the rickrack using a straight stitch and a walking foot.

3 The appliqué patterns are on page 93. Shelley and Jeanne used fusible-web appliqué, but you can prepare the following number of shapes for your favorite method of appliqué from the fabrics indicated:
- 4 sets of letters for *Merry* from black print
- 4 holly leaves from green print
- 4 stars from light gold print
- 4 berries from red print

4 Using the photo on page 90 as a guide, position and appliqué the shapes in place on the pieced background. Be sure that you leave at least 1" between the words and the raw edge of the pieced

background. If desired, use matching thread to blanket stitch around each shape by hand or machine.

5 Sew the black 1½" x 32½" strips to the long sides of the runner. Sew the black 1½" x 14½" strips to the short sides. Press the seam allowances toward the black border.

6 Sew the red 2½" x 34½" strips to the long sides of the runner. Sew the red 2½" x 18½" strips to the short sides. Press the seam allowances toward the red border.

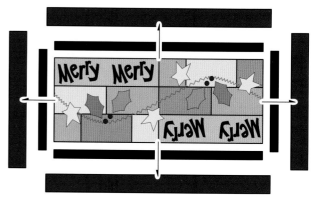

Table-runner assembly

Finishing

Go to ShopMartingale.com/HowtoQuilt if you need more information on any of the finishing steps.

1 Layer, baste, and quilt your table runner.

2 Using the black 2½"-wide strips, prepare and attach the binding.

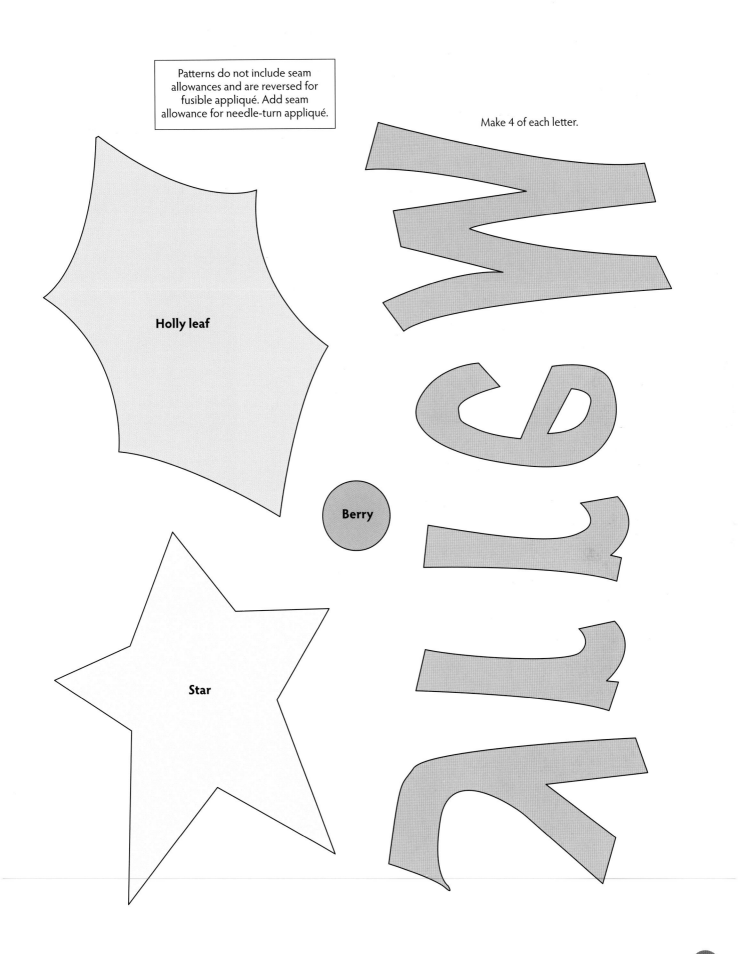

Patterns do not include seam allowances and are reversed for fusible appliqué. Add seam allowance for needle-turn appliqué.

Make 4 of each letter.

Holly leaf

Berry

Star

Rhubarb Crisp

The best way of "preserving our ties to the past," according to Jo Morton, is making "new quilts that look old." She shows the way back in time with reproduction fabrics—many of them her own designs—and with classic Sawtooth Star blocks, framed by flying-geese sashing. Loaded with old-fashioned charm, this runner brings to mind the dessert savored on the nineteenth-century homestead. You can practically smell the flavorful rhubarb baked with sugar and spice!

FINISHED RUNNER: 14" x 38" • **FINISHED BLOCK:** 4" x 4"
Designed by Jo Morton; pieced by Mary Fornoff; quilted by Bonnie Haith; bound by Sheri Dowding

Materials

Yardage is based on 42"-wide fabric.

Scraps of 12 light prints with tan, ecru, taupe, or gold as the background color for Sawtooth Star blocks

Scraps of 12 medium to dark prints with rust, brown, and black predominating for Sawtooth Star blocks

Scraps of 4 to 8 additional light prints and 4 to 8 additional dark prints for flying-geese sashing

7½" x 10" piece *each* of 2 different reddish-brown prints for cornerstones

¼ yard of brown print for binding

¾ yard of fabric for backing

18" x 42" piece of batting

Cutting

From the dark prints for flying-geese sashing, cut:
32 sets of 4 matching squares, 1⅞" x 1⅞" (128 total)

From the light prints for flying-geese sashing, cut a *total* of:
32 squares, 3¼" x 3¼"

From *each* of the 12 light prints for blocks, cut:
1 square, 3¼" x 3¼" (12 total)
4 squares, 1½" x 1½" (48 total)

From *each* of the 12 medium to dark prints for blocks, cut:
1 square, 2½" x 2½" (12 total)
4 squares, 1⅞" x 1⅞" (48 total)

From *each* of the 2 different reddish-brown prints, cut:
12 squares, 2½" x 2½" (24 total; 3 will be extra)

From the brown print, cut:
3 strips, 1¼" x 42"

Making the Flying-Geese Units

1 Draw a diagonal line on the wrong side of four matching dark 1⅞" squares.

2 Align two of these squares on opposite corners of a light 3¼" square, right sides together. The squares will overlap in the center and the drawn lines will connect. Sew ¼" from both sides of the drawn line. Cut apart on the drawn line. Press the seam allowances toward the small triangles.

3 Place a dark 1⅞" square on top of the large triangle of each unit from step 2, aligning the left side and bottom edges. Make sure the drawn diagonal line starts at the corner and ends at the center. Sew ¼" from both sides of the drawn line. Cut apart on the drawn line. Press the seam allowances toward the dark triangles. Each unit will make two flying-geese units for a total of four matching units. If necessary, trim each unit to measure 1½" x 2½".

4 Repeat steps 1–3 with the remaining light and dark pieces for flying-geese units to make a total of 128 units.

5 Sew four assorted flying-geese units together along the long edges. Repeat to make a total of 32 flying-geese sashing units.

Make 32.

Making the Sawtooth Star Blocks

1 Refer to steps 1–3 of "Making the Flying-Geese Units" to make 12 sets of four matching flying-geese units using the light 3¼" squares and dark 1⅞" squares cut for the blocks.

2 Arrange four matching flying-geese units, the matching dark 2½" square, and the four matching light 1½" squares in three horizontal rows. Sew the pieces in each row together; press the seam allowances toward the squares. Sew the rows together, nesting the seam allowances; press the seam allowances toward the center row. Repeat to make 12 Sawtooth Star blocks.

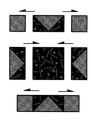

Make 12.

● JO'S CLIPPING TRICK

For a Sawtooth Star block that lies flat, on either side of the nested seam allowances, cut through both layers of the seam allowance, right up to the stitching. Press the seam allowances of the flying-geese unit toward the center and the seam allowances of the corner square outward. Press the seam-allowance intersections open.

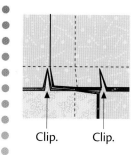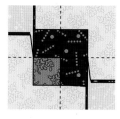

Clip. Clip.   Press open.

Assembling the Runner

1 Referring to the photo on page 94, arrange the Sawtooth Star blocks in six rows of two blocks each, leaving plenty of space between each block. Strive for a pleasing balance of colors. Place flying-geese sashing units between and on each side of the blocks, paying careful attention to the direction of the points. Fill in with the reddish brown 2½" squares. For the quilt shown, the same print was used for the squares for the center three horizontal rows and a different print was used for the squares in the two horizontal rows on each end. Reposition sashing strips as needed so the color distribution is well balanced.

2 When you're satisfied with the arrangement, pin and sew the pieces in each row together. Gently press the seam allowances toward the blocks or cornerstones; avoid stretching the sashing strips.

3 Pin and sew the rows together, matching seam intersections. Use "Jo's Clipping Trick" on page 96 at the seam intersections. Press sashing-strip seam allowances toward the block or cornerstone.

Finishing

Go to ShopMartingale.com/HowtoQuilt if you need more information on any of the finishing steps.

1 Layer, baste, and quilt your table runner.

2 Using the brown print 1¼"-wide strips, prepare and attach the binding. (The quilt shown uses single-fold binding, not double.)

Tulips and Tossed Greens

Spring has sprung in this whimsical table runner adorned with leaping rabbits, fluttering vines of blooming yo-yos, and sun-kissed tulips. Brighten any tabletop with this cheerful little quilt as you celebrate the arrival of balmy days and clear blue skies.

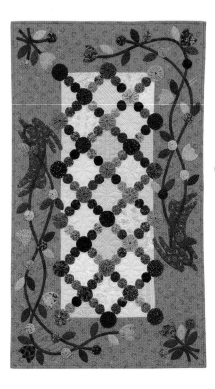

FINISHED RUNNER: 23¼" x 40⅛" • **FINISHED BLOCK:** 4" x 4"
Designed by Kim Diehl

Materials

Yardage is based on 42"-wide fabric. Fat quarters are 18" x 21".

1½ yards *total* of assorted prints for yo-yos and tulip appliqués
1⅛ yards of light green print for border and binding
⅝ yard *total* of assorted cream prints for blocks and side setting triangles
1 fat quarter of brown print for rabbit appliqués
1 fat quarter of green plaid for vine and leaf appliqués
Scraps of assorted green prints for leaf appliqués
1⅓ yards of fabric for backing
30" x 47" piece of batting
Fusible web (optional)
¼" bias bar
#8 pearl cotton in a neutral color
Size 5 embroidery needle
Straw needle
Liquid basting glue

Cutting

Appliqué patterns A–E are on page 102. Kim uses freezer-paper appliqué and machine stitching, but you can prepare the shapes for your favorite method. For more details on appliqué, go to ShopMartingale.com/HowtoQuilt for free information, or see Kim's book Simple Appliqué *(Martingale, 2015) for a variety of appliqué techniques.*

From the assorted cream prints, cut a *total* of:
13 squares, 4½" x 4½"
4 squares, 5¼" x 5¼"; cut diagonally into quarters to yield 16 triangles (2 will be extra)

From the light green print, cut:
2 strips, 6¼" x 28⅝"
2 strips, 6¼" x 23¼"
4 strips, 2½" x 42"

From the assorted prints, cut a *total* of:
28 using pattern A
102 using pattern B
10 using pattern D

From the brown print, cut:
2 using pattern C

From the green plaid, cut on the *bias* grain:
Enough 1"-wide lengths to make four 36"-long strips when joined end to end
6 strips, 1¼" x 4"

From the remainder of the green plaid and the assorted green print scraps, cut a *total* of:
40 using pattern E

Assembling the Runner

1 Arrange the cream print squares and setting triangles into five diagonal rows as shown. Join the pieces in each row. Press the seam allowances open. Trim away the dog-ear points. Join the rows. Press the seam allowances open.

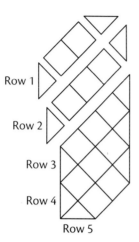

Row 1
Row 2
Row 3
Row 4
Row 5

2 Sew the remaining setting triangles into pairs to make two corner units. Press the seam allowances open. Trim away the dog-ear points. Add a corner unit to the top-left and bottom-right corners of the table-runner center. Press the seam allowances open.

3 Join the light green 6¼" x 28⅝" strips to opposite sides of the table runner. Press the seam allowances toward the green print. Join the light green 6¼" x 23¼" strips to the remaining sides. Press the seam allowances toward the green print. The pieced table-runner top should now measure 23¼" x 40⅛".

Making the Yo-Yos

1 Select an A circle. With the wrong side up, turn a portion of the edge toward you ⅛" to create a hem. Using a knotted length of pearl cotton and the size 5 embroidery needle, bring the needle up through the hem from the wrong side of the folded fabric to bury the knot between the layers. Sew a running stitch through all of the layers, close to the folded edge. Continue turning the hem to the back and stitching as you work your way around the circle to your starting position; do not cut the thread. Gently pull the threaded needle to gather the yo-yo edges into the center. Insert the needle just to the side of the center, under the gathered edge, and bring it out on the back of the yo-yo. Knot and clip the thread from the back, keeping the gathers taut. Repeat for a total of 28 large yo-yos.

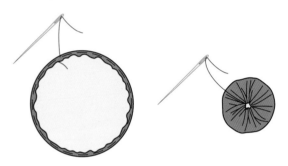

2 Repeat step 1 with the B circles for a total of 102 small yo-yos.

Appliquéing the Runner

1 Center a large yo-yo on each corner of the cream squares and at the points of each setting triangle. When you're pleased with their placement, use two or three drops of liquid basting glue to anchor each yo-yo in place.

2 Position two small yo-yos on the cream-print seamlines (but not on the border edges), centering them to fill the spaces between the large yo-yos. Anchor the small yo-yos with liquid basting glue. Reserve the remaining 22 small yo-yos.

3 Use the straw needle and matching thread to stitch the yo-yos in place.

4 Position a C appliqué onto one long side of the border as shown; baste. Appliqué the shape in place, leaving small openings as shown so the vines can be added later. Repeat on the opposite border.

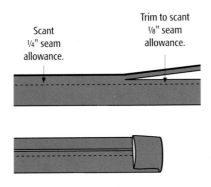

Leave open.

Leave open.

5 Join the 1"-wide bias lengths of green plaid end to end to make four segments, each 36" long. With wrong sides together, fold each green plaid 36" and 4" bias segment in half lengthwise and use a scant ¼" seam allowance to stitch along the long raw edges to form a tube. Slide the bias bar through each tube to easily press it flat, centering the seam allowance so that it will be hidden from the front of the finished stem. (If the seam allowance will be visible, trim it to a scant ⅛".) Fold one end of each 4" stem under about ¼" and anchor it with liquid basting glue.

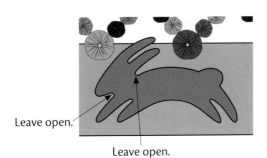

Scant ¼" seam allowance.

Trim to scant ⅛" seam allowance.

6 Using the photo on page 98 as a guide, lay out and baste a prepared 36" vine, tucking one raw end under a rabbit opening and shaping the vine to flow around the border corner; trim any unnecessary length. In the same manner, lay out and baste a second prepared vine, tucking one raw end under the remaining rabbit opening. Appliqué the vines in place. Appliqué the unstitched areas of the rabbit. Repeat with the remaining rabbit appliqué.

7 Referring to the photo, work from the bottom layer to the top to lay out and secure nine reserved yo-yos, 15 E appliqués, and four D appliqués along the vines of one rabbit. Repeat with the remaining rabbit appliqué.

8 In each open border corner, lay out, baste, and stitch three 4" bias stems. To the stems in each corner, stitch four E appliqués, two reserved yo-yos, and one D appliqué.

Finishing

Go to ShopMartingale.com/HowtoQuilt if you need more information on any of the finishing steps.

1 Layer, baste, and quilt your table runner.

2 Using the light green 2½"-wide strips, prepare and attach the binding.

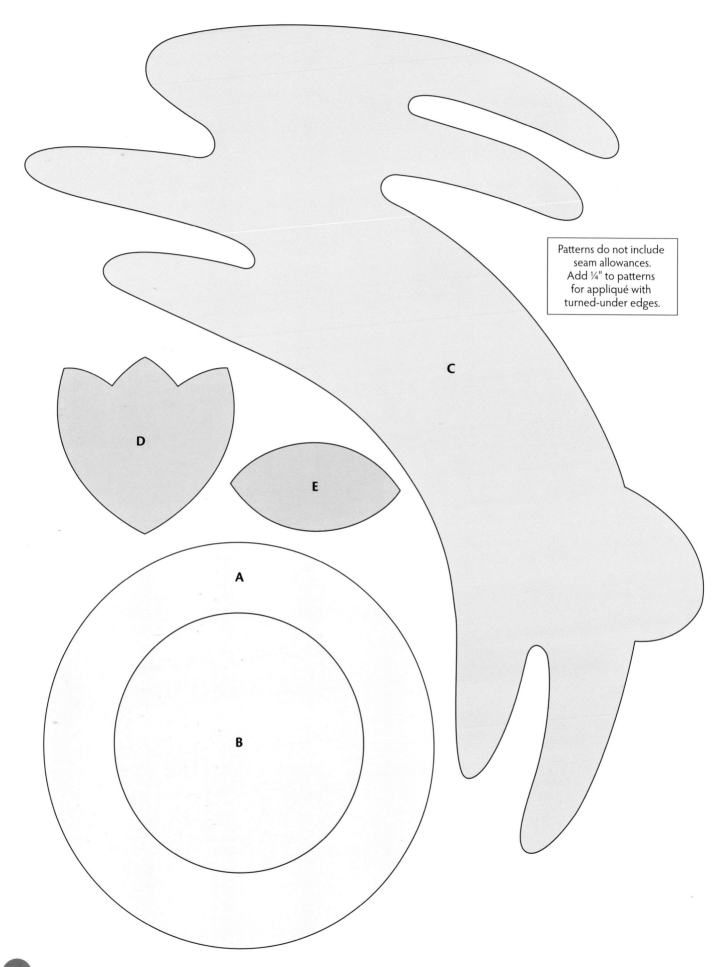

Patterns do not include
seam allowances.
Add ¼" to patterns
for appliqué with
turned-under edges.

Toyland

Candy-themed fabrics are highlighted in this yuletide runner. You can choose similar fabrics or look for motifs with toys, animals, pinecones, or any Christmas-themed print. With simple construction methods, the trees and little Cabin blocks are fun to create, and sure to be a staple of your holiday decorating for many years to come.

FINISHED RUNNER: 14½" x 70" • **FINISHED BLOCK:** 6" x 6"

Designed and made by Mary Hickey

Materials

Yardage is based on 42"-wide fabric. Fat eighths are 9" x 21".

⅞ yard of dark red print for Cabin blocks, 2nd and 4th borders, and binding

⅝ yard of red-and-white print for 3rd border

½ yard of green plaid for sashing and 1st border

½ yard of white print for block backgrounds

⅛ yard *each* of 3 assorted green prints for Tree blocks

1 fat eighth of dark green stripe for Cabin blocks

1 fat eighth of brown print for Tree blocks

Scraps of red-and-white stripe for windows and doors

1¼ yards of fabric for backing

19" x 74" piece of batting

2 small red tassels (optional)

Template plastic

Cutting

From the white print, cut:

1 strip, 3½" x 42"; crosscut into:
    4 squares, 3½" x 3½"
    4 rectangles, 1" x 3½"

2 strips, 2¼" x 42"; crosscut into
    24 squares, 2¼" x 2¼"

1 strip, 2¼" x 42"; crosscut into:
    8 rectangles, 1¾" x 2¼"
    8 rectangles, 1" x 2¼"

1 strip, 1¾" x 20"

2 strips, 3" x 8"

From the assorted green prints, cut a *total* of:

4 rectangles, 2¼" x 4"
4 rectangles, 2¼" x 5½"
4 rectangles, 2¼" x 6½"

From the brown print, cut:

1 strip, 1½" x 8"

From the dark green stripe, cut:

2 rectangles, 3½" x 6½"

Continued on page 105

Continued from page 103

From the dark red print, cut:

5 strips, 2½" x 42"

8 strips, 1" x 42"; crosscut 2 of the strips into:
    2 strips, 1" x 15"
    4 strips, 1" x 11"

1 strip, 1¾" x 20"

2 rectangles, 1½" x 2"

2 squares, 1½" x 1½"

4 rectangles, 1" x 3½"

2 rectangles, 1" x 1½"

From the scraps of red-and-white stripe, cut:

2 squares, 1½" x 1½"

2 rectangles, 1½" x 2½"

From the green plaid, cut:

3 strips, 2" x 42"

1 strip, 2½" x 42"; crosscut into 6 rectangles, 2½" x 6½"

1 square, 6½" x 6½"

From the red-and-white print, cut:

3 strips, 2¼" x 42"

1 square, 10" x 10"; cut in half diagonally to yield
    2 triangles

Making the Tree Blocks

1. Using a pencil and your rotary-cutting ruler, draw a diagonal line from corner to corner on the wrong side of each white 2¼" square. With right sides together, place a marked square on the left end of each green 2¼" x 4" rectangle, with the drawn line going from the lower-left corner to the top edge of the rectangle. Stitch on the marked lines. Trim ¼" from the stitching line. Press the seam allowances toward the green rectangles. Repeat on the opposite end of the green rectangles, reversing the direction of the stitching line. Repeat to sew a marked white square on each end of the green 2¼" x 5½" rectangles and the green 2¼" x 6½" rectangles. You will have four of each unit.

2. Stitch a white 1¾" x 2¼" rectangle on each short end of a 4" tree unit. Press the seam allowances toward the white rectangles. Stitch a white 1" x 2¼" rectangle on each short end of a 5½" tree unit. Press the seam allowances toward the white rectangles. Make four of each unit.

3. Sew the brown 1½" x 8" strip between the two white 3" x 8" strips. Press the seam allowances toward the brown strip. Crosscut the strip set into four segments, 1¼" wide, to make four trunk units.

4. Stitch one of each tree unit and one trunk segment together to make a block as shown. Press the seam allowances downward. Make four Tree blocks.

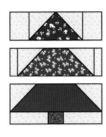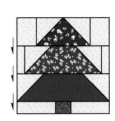

Make 4.

Making the Cabin Blocks

1. Using a pencil and your rotary-cutting ruler, draw a diagonal line from corner to corner on the wrong side of each white 3½" square. With right sides together, place a marked square on the left end of each dark green stripe 3½" x 6½" rectangle, with the drawn line going from the lower-left corner to the top edge of the rectangle. Stitch on the marked lines. Trim ¼" from the stitching line. Press the seam allowances toward the green rectangles. Repeat on the opposite end of the green rectangles, reversing the direction of the stitching line. Make two roof units.

2. Stitch the white and dark red 1¾" x 20" strips together along the long edges. Press the seam allowances in one direction. Make a plastic template of triangle A on page 107, and place the template with the angled line exactly on the seamline of the strip set. Cut two units with the template in one position, then flip the template over, repositioning it as before, and cut two reversed units. (Don't worry that the grain line will be on the partial bias when stitched into the Cabin blocks.)

3. To make the door unit, stitch a dark red 1½" square and a red-stripe 1½" x 2½" rectangle together. Press the seam allowances toward the square. Make two door units.

4 To make the window unit, stitch a dark red 1" x 1½" rectangle, a red-stripe 1½" square, and a dark red 1½" x 2" rectangle together. Press the seam allowances away from the square. Make two window units.

5 Arrange one unit each from steps 1–4, two dark red 1" x 3½" rectangles, and two white 1" x 3½" rectangles as shown. Stitch the cabin pieces together in a horizontal row, pressing as indicated. Then stitch the cabin unit and roof unit together to complete the block. Press the seam allowances upward. Make two Cabin blocks.

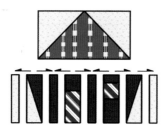

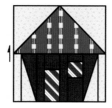

Make 2.

Assembling the Runner

1 Arrange the blocks, six green plaid 2½" x 6½" rectangles, and the green plaid 6½" square in one column as shown. Stitch the pieces together and press the seam allowances toward the green plaid sashing.

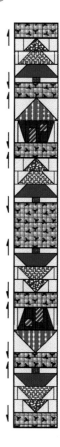

2 Join the three green plaid 2"-wide strips end to end. From the pieced strip, cut two strips to fit the length of the table-runner center and stitch them to each of the long sides.

3 Repeat step 2 to measure, cut, and sew the dark red 1"-wide strips, then the red-and-white 2¼"-wide strips, and lastly the remaining dark red 1"-wide strips.

4 Stitch one dark red 1" x 15" strip to each end of the runner top; press.

5 Sew red 1" x 11" strips to both short sides of each red-and-white triangle and trim as shown. Sew a triangle to each end of the runner top; press.

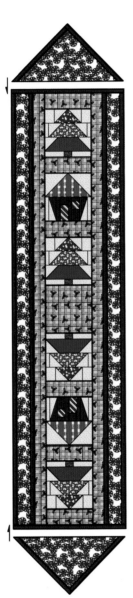

Assembly diagram

Finishing

Go to ShopMartingale.com/HowtoQuilt if you need more information on any of the finishing steps.

1 Layer, baste, and quilt your table runner.

2 Using the dark red 2½"-wide strips, prepare and attach the binding.

3 Hand stitch a tassel to each end of the runner, if desired.

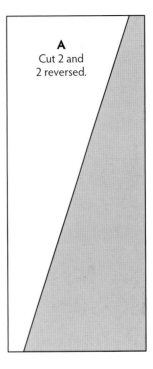

A
Cut 2 and
2 reversed.

Pinwheels

Pinwheels is loosely based on the easiest of blocks, the Courthouse Steps version of the traditional Log Cabin. Terry's new "spin" is a welcome change from the typical Pinwheel that requires matching eight seams in the center of the block. Here, there are no center seams to match. Fabric logs compose and frame the block, build the setting triangles, and cap the pointed ends. These Pinwheels are a breeze!

FINISHED RUNNER: 15⅛" x 52⅛" • **FINISHED BLOCK:** 11" x 11"
Designed and made by Terry Atkinson

Materials

Yardage is based on 42"-wide fabric. Fat quarters are 18" x 21"; a fat eighth is 9" x 21".

8 fat quarters of assorted colorful prints for blocks, setting triangles, and binding
1 fat quarter of white print for blocks
1 fat eighth of yellow print for blocks
⅞ yard of fabric for backing
19" x 56" piece of batting

Cutting

From *each of 3* prints, cut:
1 strip, 1¾" x 21"; crosscut into:
    2 rectangles, 1¾" x 4½" (6 total)
    2 rectangles, 1¾" x 2" (6 total)
4 squares, 2½" x 2½" (12 total)

From *each of 3* remaining colorful prints, cut:
2 strips, 1¾" x 21" (6 total);
    crosscut each strip into:
    1 strip, 1¾" x 8½" (6 total)
    1 strip, 1¾" x 11" (6 total)

From the remaining yardage of the 8 colorful prints, cut a *total* of:*
24 strips, 1¾" x 21"; crosscut into:
    8 strips, 1¾" x 12" (H)
    8 strips, 1¾" x 11" (G)
    4 strips, 1¾" x 9½" (F)
    4 strips, 1¾" x 8½" (E)
    4 strips, 1¾" x 7" (D)
    4 strips, 1¾" x 6" (C)
    4 strips, 1¾" x 4½" (B)
    4 strips, 1¾" x 3½" (A)
8 strips, 2¼" x 21"

From the yellow print, cut:
3 squares, 2" x 2"
1 square, 3½" x 3½"; cut into
    quarters diagonally to yield
    4 triangles

From the white print, cut:
5 strips, 2½" x 21"; crosscut into:
    12 rectangles, 2½" x 4½"
    12 squares, 2½" x 2½"

*Cutting the longer pieces first ensures you will have enough fabric.

Making the Blocks

1 Stitch matching colorful 1¾" x 2" rectangles to the top and bottom edges of a yellow 2" square; press. Stitch 1¾" x 4½" rectangles in the same print to the sides; press.

2 Use a pencil to mark a diagonal line on the wrong side of four matching colorful print 2½" squares. With right sides together and raw edges aligned, place a marked square on a white 2½" square. Stitch directly on the marked line. Trim ¼" beyond the stitching line; press. Make two.

3 Sew a white 2½" square to each unit from step 2, taking care to orient the unit as shown; press. Make two.

Make 2.

4 Place a remaining marked colorful 2½" square on the corner of a white 2½" x 4½" rectangle. Stitch, trim, and press. Make two.

Stitch.   Trim.   Press.

5 Sew a white 2½" x 4½" rectangle and a unit from step 4 together as shown; press. Make two.

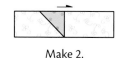

Make 2.

6 Sew units from step 3 to the top and bottom of the unit from step 1 as shown; press. Sew units from step 5 to the sides; press.

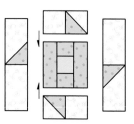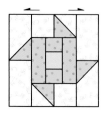

7 Sew matching 1¾" x 8½" strips of one of three colorful prints to the top and bottom of the unit from step 6; press. Sew 1¾" x 11" strips in the same print to the sides; press.

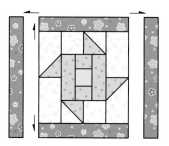

8 Repeat steps 1–7 to make a total of three Pinwheel blocks, each using different-colored prints.

Making the Setting Triangles

You will use the 1¾"-wide assorted colorful strips in varying lengths (strips A–H) to make the Log Cabin setting triangles. Refer to the photo on page 108 as needed.

1 Sew an A strip to one short side of a yellow quarter-square triangle; press. Sew a B strip to the adjacent short side of the unit; press. Add strips C, D, E, F, G, and H, alternating the same two sides of the quarter-square triangle as shown. Press the seam allowances toward each newly added strip as you go, and then apply spray starch and press the finished unit.

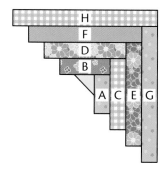

2 Use a ruler and a pencil to measure 11⅞" from the 90° corner of the step 1 unit along both adjacent edges. Draw a diagonal line connecting the two points. Stay stitch ¼" *inside* the drawn line, and then trim directly on the drawn line.

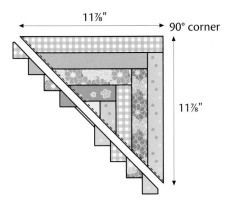

Stay stitch and trim.

3 Repeat steps 1 and 2 to make a total of four setting triangles. Set the remaining G and H strips aside for now. You will use them later to complete the runner top.

Assembling the Runner

1 Arrange the Pinwheel blocks and setting triangles as shown in the assembly diagram at right.

2 Sew two remaining G and H strips to two sides of the top and bottom Pinwheel blocks, alternating G, H, G, and H as shown. Press the seam allowances toward each newly added strip as you go.

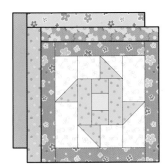

3 Sew the blocks and setting triangles together in diagonal rows as shown; press.

4 Sew the rows together; press. Trim the corners of the top and bottom Pinwheel blocks even with the sides of the runner top.

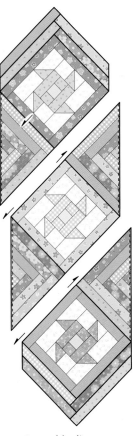

Assembly diagram

Finishing

Go to ShopMartingale.com/HowtoQuilt if you need more information on any of the finishing steps.

1 Layer, baste, and quilt your table runner.

2 Using the colorful 2¼"-wide strips, prepare and attach the binding.

Rungs

Karla Alexander, author of popular Stack the Deck *and other great titles, was eager to adapt her clever speed-piecing technique to this long, lean piece. Here, she shares her steps for cutting blocks and strips and reshuffling the deck of fabrics to make surprising and wonderful strip-set blocks. Then, the blocks are simply joined end to end. Scale your "ladder" to fit your table. Customize your colors, too, making sure to choose ones with great contrast.*

FINISHED RUNNER: 16" x 60"
Designed and made by Karla Alexander

Materials

Yardage is based on 42"-wide fabric.

¼ yard *each* of 3 different green prints for blocks

¼ yard *each* of 3 different medium to dark purple batiks for blocks

⅜ yard of bright accent print for binding

1⅞ yards of fabric for backing

20" x 65" piece of batting

● PUNCH IT UP!

For an unexpected finish, introduce a totally different accent color for the binding—like the hot pink print used here.

Cutting

From *each* of the 3 green prints, cut:

1 rectangle, 7½" x 17" (3 total)
1 rectangle, 5" x 17" (3 total)

From *each* of the 3 purple batiks, cut:

1 rectangle, 7½" x 17" (3 total)
1 rectangle, 5" x 17" (3 total)

From the bright accent print, cut:

4 strips, 2½" x 42"

Making the Blocks

1 Stack the six 7½" x 17" rectangles right side up, alternating purple and green fabrics. Make sure all the edges are perfectly aligned.

2 Turn the stack so the short edges are on the left and right. Measure and cut 3" from each side.

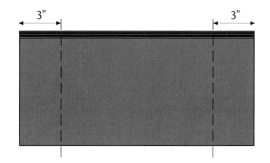

3 Peel off the top layer of the left 3" section and shuffle it to the bottom of the stack.

4 Peel off the top three layers of the right 3" section and shuffle them to the bottom of the stack.

5 Sew the three pieces of each layer together. Press the seam allowances toward the purple fabrics.

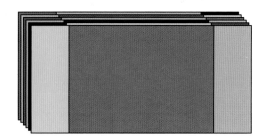

6 Crosscut each layer into one of each of the following width segments: 1", 1½", 2", and 3".

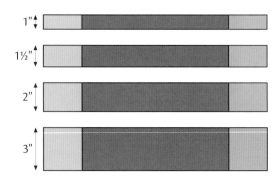

7 Repeat steps 1–5 *only* with the six 5" x 17" rectangles.

Assembling the Runner

1 Arrange the segments into six units of five segments each as desired or follow the list below. Alternate purple and green centers in each unit. Pin the segments in each unit together, nesting the seam allowances for corners that meet perfectly.

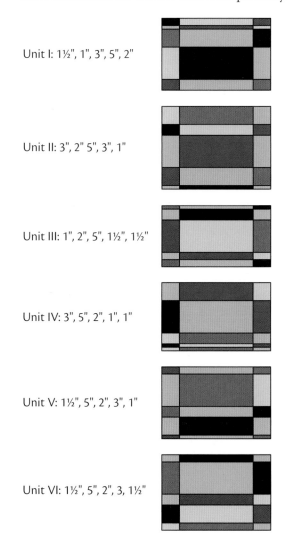

Unit I: 1½", 1", 3", 5", 2"

Unit II: 3", 2" 5", 3", 1"

Unit III: 1", 2", 5", 1½", 1½"

Unit IV: 3", 5", 2", 1", 1"

Unit V: 1½", 5", 2", 3", 1"

Unit VI: 1½", 5", 2", 3, 1½"

2 Sew the segments in each unit together. Alternate the sewing direction as you add each new segment. Press seam allowances toward the darker center sections. Sew the units together.

● DARE TO BE DIFFERENT

For a look different from the one shown, you can cut different-width segments in steps 2 and 6 of "Making the Blocks," but be sure no segments are narrower than 1".

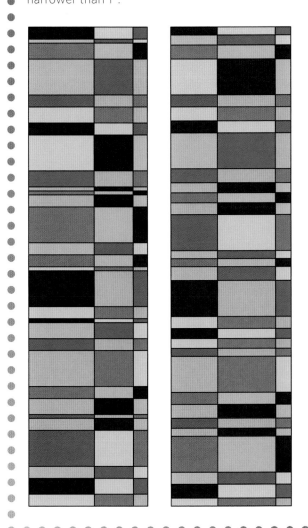

Finishing

Go to ShopMartingale.com/HowtoQuilt if you need more information on any of the finishing steps.

1 Layer, baste, and quilt your table runner.

2 Using the bright print 2½"-wide strips, prepare and attach the binding.

It's a Celebration

Everyone loves a celebration, right? Break out the party ware and set the table for some fun! Birthdays, Cinco de Mayo, graduations—whatever the occasion, this brightly colored runner and matching place mats will help you kick the festivities into high gear.

FINISHED RUNNER: 20½" x 50½" • **FINISHED PLACE MAT:** 12½" x 18½"
Designed and made by Jackie Kunkel

Materials

Yardage is based on 42"-wide fabric and is sufficient to make 1 table runner and 6 place mats.

⅓ yard *each* of 11 assorted black prints for blocks and borders

¼ yard *each* of 11 assorted white prints for blocks and borders

19 strips, 2½" x 21", of assorted bright prints for blocks and table-runner corner squares

1⅛ yards of multicolored stripe for binding

3¾ yards of fabric for backing

6 pieces, 18" x 24", of batting for place mats

1 piece, 28" x 58", of batting for table runner

Template plastic

Cutting

From *each* of the assorted white prints, cut:

1 strip, 2½" x 42"; crosscut into
  2 strips, 2½" x 21" (22 total; 3 will be extra)
1 strip, 4½" x 42" (11 total)

From *each* of the assorted black prints, cut:

1 strip, 4½" x 42" (11 total)

From the remainder of the assorted black prints, cut a *total* of:

12 strips, 1½" x 42"; crosscut 9 of the strips into:
  14 strips, 1½" x 10½"
  12 strips, 1½" x 14½"

From the multicolored stripe, cut:

15 strips, 2¼" x 42"

Making the Units and Triangles

1 Pair a white 2½"-wide strip with a bright strip. With right sides together, sew the strips together along their long edges. Press the seam allowances toward the bright strip. Repeat to make a total of 19 strip sets. Cut the strip sets into 2½"-wide segments, for a total of 148; you'll need 58 segments for the table runner and 90 segments for the place mats (15 for each mat).

2 Select five assorted segments from step 1. Lay them out as shown on page 118, making sure the bright squares create a checkerboard pattern. Sew the segments together to make a checkerboard unit. Press the seam allowances in one direction. Make 10 units for the table runner and 18 units for the place mats (3 for each

mat). You'll have eight segments left over to make Four Patch corner squares for the table runner.

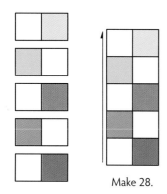

Make 28.

3 Trace the triangle pattern on page 119 onto template plastic and cut out on the marked lines.

4 Using the triangle template and the 4½"-wide strips of black and white prints, trace 116 black and 116 white pieces. Use a rotary cutter and ruler to cut out the pieces.

Assembling the Runner

1 Sew 10 units together as shown to make the table runner. Press the seam allowances in one direction. The table runner should measure 10½" x 40½".

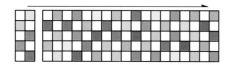

2 Sew a black 1½" x 10½" strip to each short end of the runner. Press the seam allowances toward the black strips. Join the three black 1½" x 42" strips end to end to make a strip at least 86" long. From the pieced strip, cut two 42½"-long strips and sew them to the long sides of the table runner. Press the seam allowances toward the black strips. The table runner should measure 12½" x 42½".

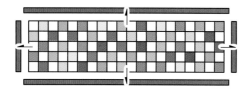

3 Place the table runner on a design wall and arrange 26 black and 26 white triangles along each long side, alternating the pieces as shown. Then place eight black and eight white triangles on each short side. Rearrange the triangles until you are pleased with the appearance. Sew the triangles in each row together to make a border strip. Press the seam allowances in one direction. Trim the 16-piece border strips to measure 12½" long. Trim the 52-piece border strips to measure 42½" long.

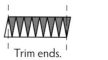

Trim ends.   Make 2.

Make 2.

⬤ JOINING THE PIECES

To join the triangles, place black and white pieces right sides together, offsetting them so you can see little "dog ears" overhanging each piece. Offsetting the triangles will allow you to sew straight border strips.

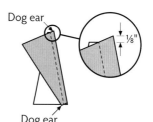

Dog ear

⅛"

Dog ear

4 Lay out two of the remaining segments from step 2 of "Making the Units and Triangles" as shown. Join the segments to make a Four Patch block. Press the seam allowances in one direction. Make a total of four blocks.

Make 4.

5 Sew the 12½"-long border strips to the short sides of the table runner. Press the seam allowances toward the inner border. Sew Four Patch blocks to the ends of each 42½"-long border strip and press the seam allowances toward the Four Patch blocks. Sew these borders to the long sides of the table runner. Press the seam allowances toward the inner border.

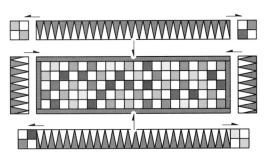

Table-runner layout

Assembling the Place Mats

1 For each place mat, sew three units together as shown. Press the seam allowances in one direction. Each place mat should measure 10½" x 12½". Make a total of six.

Make 6.

2 Sew black 1½" x 10½" strips to the short ends of each place mat. Press the seam allowances toward the black strips. Then sew black 1½" x 14½" strips to the long edges of each place mat. Press the seam allowances toward the black strips. Each place mat should measure 12½" x 14½". Make a total of six.

3 For each place mat, position eight black and eight white triangles on one short side of the mat, alternating the black and white pieces as shown in the place-mat layout. Sew the triangles together to make a border strip. Press the seam allowances in one direction. Trim the border strip to measure 12½" long. Make six border strips.

4 Sew a border strip from step 3 to one short side of each place mat. Press the seam allowances toward the inner border.

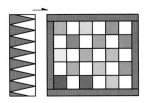

Place-mat layout

Finishing

Go to ShopMartingale.com/HowtoQuilt if you need more information on any of the finishing steps.

1 Layer, baste, and quilt your table runner and place mats.

2 Using the multicolored-stripe 2¼"-wide strips, prepare and attach the binding.

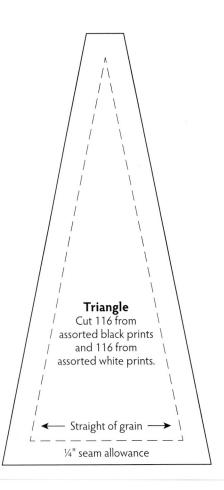

Triangle
Cut 116 from assorted black prints and 116 from assorted white prints.

◄— Straight of grain —►

¼" seam allowance

Outback Sunset

As a quilting celeb in the land Down Under, Judy Hooworth regularly turns traditional quilt blocks on their heads. Here, she cuts triangles from strip sets, producing groups of "tops" and "tails." Tops combine for one block, tails for a second, so, as Judy says, "Simplicity is the order of the day." But she also incorporates bold geometric prints and ingenious Xs, and the outcome is hot, hot, hot—like the colors of the canyons and the evening skies at Australia's Red Center.

FINISHED RUNNER: 18" x 80"
Designed and made by Judy Hooworth

Materials

Yardage is based on 42"-wide fabric.

⅝ yard of red-and-black stripe for border

⅓ yard of turquoise print for blocks and binding

⅓ yard *each* of yellow, red, and black prints for blocks

¼ yard of black-and-white stripe for blocks

¼ yard of purple print for blocks

¼ yard of red-and-black dot for border

2½ yards of fabric for backing

22" x 84" piece of batting

12" (or larger) square ruler with 45°-angle line

Cutting

From *each* of the red and black prints, cut:

4 strips, 2¼" x 42" (8 total)

From the yellow print, cut:

4 strips, 2⅜" x 42"

From the black-and-white stripe, cut:

4 strips, 1½" x 42"; crosscut into 12 identical strips, 1½" x 9"

From the turquoise print, cut:

6 strips, 1½" x 42"; crosscut 1 strip into 7 squares, 1½" x 1½"

From the purple print, cut:

4 strips, 1½" x 42"; crosscut into:
8 strips, 1½" x 9"
4 strips, 1½" x 10"

From the red-and-black stripe, cut:

4 strips, 3½" x 42"

1 strip, 2¾" x 42"; crosscut into 4 strips, 2¾" x 9"

From the red-and-black dot, cut:

1 square, 6½" x 6½"; cut in half diagonally to yield 2 triangles

1 square, 6" x 6"; cut into quarters diagonally to yield 4 triangles

Making the Blocks

1 Sew a black, a red, and a yellow print strip together along the long edges to make a strip set. Repeat to make a total of four strip sets. Press the seam allowances toward the black strips.

Make 4.

2 Trim the right-hand end of each strip set at a 45° angle, placing the 45°-angle line of the ruler at the top of the strip. Note: If you are left-handed, begin by trimming and cutting from the left end of the strip set and work in reverse from the instructions and diagrams.

3 Rotate the strip set on the cutting mat so that the cut edge is on your left and the black strip is on the bottom. Position the "0" corner of the ruler at the top of the strip, aligning the edge of the ruler with the diagonal cut. The 8¼" mark should be lined up with the bottom of the strip. Cut along the right edge of the ruler.

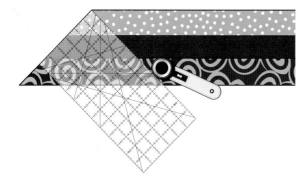

4 Turn the ruler around and cut a second triangle. Repeat the turning and cutting to cut six triangles from the strip. You will have three triangles with the black print on the longest edge of the triangle (A) and three triangles with the yellow print on the longest edge of the triangle

(B). Repeat with the remaining strip sets to cut a total of 12 A triangles and 12 B triangles. You will have two left over for another project.

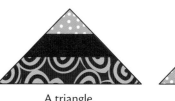

A triangle.
Cut 12.

B triangle.
Cut 12. Discard 2.

5 Lay out four A triangles, four black-and-white striped sashing strips, and one turquoise square as shown. Make sure the same-colored stripe meets the center square. Sew the pieces together, stitching from the tip to the base of the triangles where applicable. The sashing strips will extend beyond the base of the triangles. Press the seam allowances toward the sashing strips. Trim the ends of the sashing strips even with the sides of the block. Repeat to make a total of three A blocks.

A block.
Make 3.

6 Repeat step 5 to make two B blocks using the B triangles, the purple 1½" x 9" strips, and the turquoise squares.

B block.
Make 2.

Making the Pieced End Triangles

1 Sew a purple 1½" x 10" strip to one short side of each of the two remaining B triangles. The ends of the purple strips will extend beyond the base of the triangle. Press the seam allowances toward the purple strips.

2 Sew a turquoise square to one end of each of the remaining purple strips. Sew these strips to the opposite short side of the triangle, matching seams. Press the seam allowances toward the purple strips. Trim the ends of the purple strips even with the base of the B triangles.

Make 2.

Assembling the Runner

1 Alternately join the A and B blocks into one column. Center and stitch a pieced end triangle to each end. Trim the sides of the end triangles even with the sides of the joined blocks.

2 For the borders, layer the red-and-black striped 2¾" x 9" strips in pairs, wrong sides together. Cut one end of each pair at a 45° angle. Sew a strip on each side of the end triangles, with the angled end even with the sides of the table runner. Trim across the top of the end triangles, ¼" from the center of the turquoise square.

3 Stitch a red-and-black dot half-square triangle to the top of each end triangle. Trim the sides even with the angled sides of the table runner.

triangle up and trim away the striped border fabric ¼" from the stitching line.

MAKING YOUR POINT EXACTLY

Before you add each half-square triangle, fold it in half from the base to the point and press lightly to crease. When you pin the base to one end of the runner, make sure the crease aligns with the point of the joining square directly below it.

4 Stitch two red-and-black striped 3½" x 42" strips together end to end to make one long strip. Repeat with the remaining two strips. Measure the long sides of the runner top and cut each pieced strip to this measurement. Draw a line 3" from the ends of each strip.

6 Stitch these strips to the sides of the runner top, offsetting the seamline of the red-and-black triangles on the border strips with the outermost seamline of the purple strips by ¼" so that the seams match when sewn together. Press the seam allowances toward the border. Trim the red-and-black dot triangles at the end of each side border even with the top and side edges.

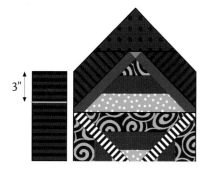

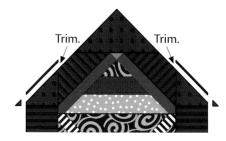

5 With right sides together, align one short edge of each red-and-black dot quarter-square triangle with the drawn lines on each strip as shown and the other short edge with the long inner edge of the border strip (the triangle is wider than the border-strip width at this point; the excess will be trimmed later). Stitch ¼" from the short edge that is aligned with the marked line. Press the

Finishing

Go to ShopMartingale.com/HowtoQuilt if you need more information on any of the finishing steps.

1 Layer, baste, and quilt your table runner.

2 Using the turquoise-print 1½"-wide strips, prepare and attach the binding. (Judy used single-fold binding, not double-fold.)

Candy Canes

Fast and easy to make, this table runner is perfect to set the mood for a Christmas celebration. Scrappy prairie points finish the edges and bright-red fabrics create a visual pop.

FINISHED RUNNER: 15" x 43"
Designed and made by Cheryl Almgren Taylor

Materials

Yardage is based on 42"-wide fabric.

½ yard *total* of assorted red prints for prairie-point border

⅜ yard of white print for center background

¼ yard of green batik for bow appliqués and inner border

Scraps of white and assorted red prints for candy-cane appliqués

1 yard of fabric for backing

16" x 44" piece of batting

Fusible web (optional)

Cutting

From the white print, cut:
1 rectangle, 11" x 39"

From the green batik, cut:
3 strips, 1½" x 42"

From the assorted red prints for the prairie-point border, cut a *total* of:
52 squares, 3" x 3"

Assembling the Runner

1 Using the patterns on page 128, prepare the appliqué pieces. Cheryl used fusible-web appliqué, but you can use your preferred method.

2 Equally space the candy-cane units on the white rectangle, leaving at least ½" of space at each end. Appliqué the units in place.

3 If desired, finish the raw edges of each appliqué piece using a machine blanket stitch, zigzag stitch, or satin stitch.

4 Trim the center panel to 10½" x 38½".

5 Sew the green 1½"-wide strips end to end to create one long strip. Measure the length of the runner through the center. Cut two green strips to fit, and sew them to the long sides of the runner top. Press the seam allowances toward the border strips.

6 Measure the width of the runner through the center, including the borders just added. Cut two green strips to fit, and sew them to the short sides of the runner top. Press the seam allowances toward the border strips.

Finishing

Go to ShopMartingale.com/HowtoQuilt if you need more information on any of the finishing steps.

1 Layer, baste, and quilt your table runner, making sure that your quilting stitches stop at least ½" from the edges of the table-runner top to allow room for attaching the prairie points and turning under the seam allowances.

2 To make the prairie points, fold each red 3" square in half diagonally, wrong sides together; press. Fold the triangles in half again; press.

Make 52.

3 Fold the backing fabric away from the edges of the table-runner top. Randomly arrange 20 prairie points along the long edges of the table-runner top, aligning the base of the triangles with the raw edge of the runner. Slip the fold of one point into the opening of the previous point, making sure the points are evenly spaced; pin in place. In the same manner, arrange six prairie points along each short end. Using a ¼" seam allowance, sew through the table-runner top and batting, sewing the prairie points in place. Do not catch the backing fabric in the seam.

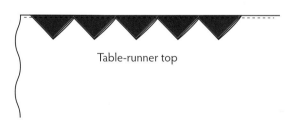

Table-runner top

4 Trim the batting close to the stitching. Fold the prairie points out, turning the seam allowance in toward the batting, and lightly press from the right side. Trim the backing fabric so that it extends ⅜" beyond the edges of the table-runner top. Turn the seam allowance of the backing under, covering the seam allowance and the machine stitches of the prairie points. Hand stitch the backing in place.

Table-runner assembly

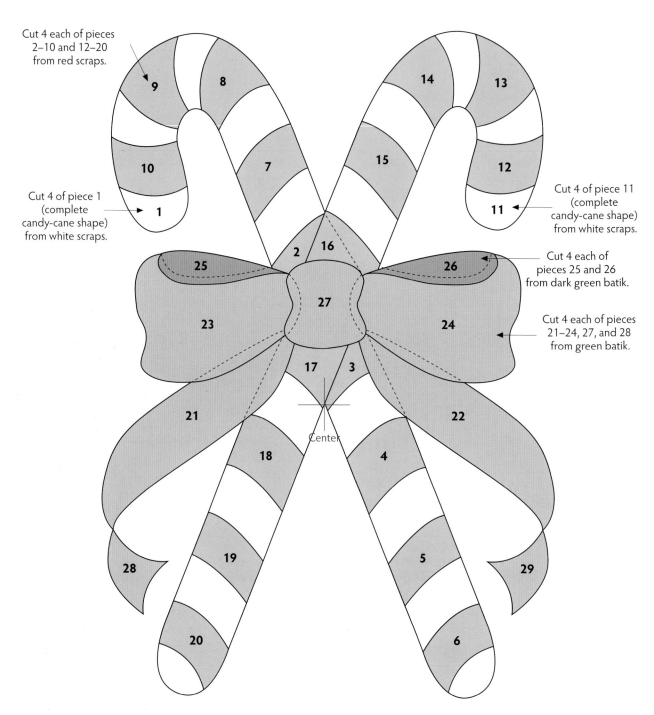

Cut 4 each of pieces 2–10 and 12–20 from red scraps.

Cut 4 of piece 1 (complete candy-cane shape) from white scraps.

Cut 4 of piece 11 (complete candy-cane shape) from white scraps.

Cut 4 each of pieces 25 and 26 from dark green batik.

Cut 4 each of pieces 21–24, 27, and 28 from green batik.

Center

Candy-cane appliqué patterns and placement diagram

Patterns are reversed for fusible appliqué and do not include seam allowances.

Berry Easy

This quick and easy table topper is a must for any picnic table! Bright, cheerful, and fast, it will be done long before the baked beans and potato salad are ready. On second thought, maybe not that fast, but still faster than getting the kids to set the table!

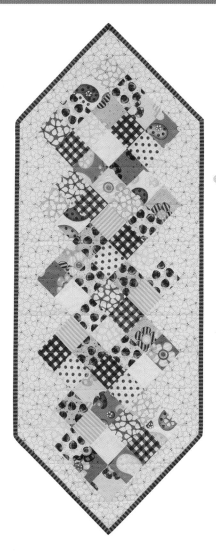

FINISHED RUNNER: 15" x 39" • **FINISHED BLOCK:** 4" x 4"
Designed and made by Mary Jacobson and Barbara Groves

Materials

Yardage is based on 42"-wide fabric. Charm squares are 5" x 5".

16 charm squares of coordinating prints for blocks
½ yard of light print for setting triangles and setting rectangles
¼ yard of blue stripe for binding
1½ yards of fabric for backing
23" x 47" piece of batting

Cutting

From the light print, cut:

1 strip, 10" x 42"; crosscut into 2 squares, 10" x 10". Cut each square into quarters diagonally to yield 8 triangles.
2 strips, 2" x 42"; crosscut into:
    2 rectangles, 2" x 12"
    2 rectangles, 2" x 14"

From the blue stripe, cut:

3 strips, 2¼" x 42"

Making the Blocks

1 Divide the 16 coordinating 5" squares into eight pairs of contrasting colors or contrasting values (light and dark).

2 Layer the pairs of squares right sides together and, using ¼" seam allowance, stitch along two opposite sides of the squares as shown.

3 Cut down the center of the squares as shown and press the seam allowances open. Repeat to make a total of 16 two-patch units.

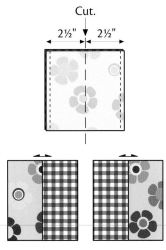

Make 16.

4 Divide the 16 two-patch units into eight *new* combinations of contrasting pairs.

5 With right sides together, layer the two-patch units, aligning the seams. Using a ¼" seam allowance, stitch along

two opposite sides, making sure to stitch across the previous seamlines as shown.

6 Cut down the center of the sewn units as shown and press the seam allowances open. The blocks should now measure 4½" x 4½". Make 16 blocks.

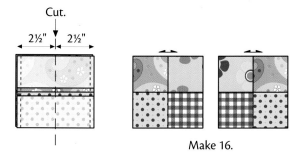

Make 16.

Assembling the Runner

1 Arrange and sew the Four Patch blocks and setting triangles together in diagonal rows. Trim the excess from the points of the triangles. Sew the rows together.

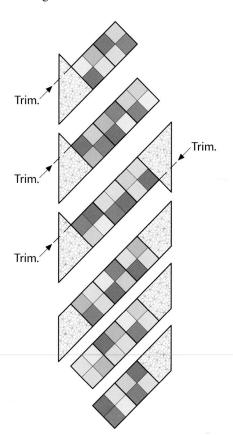

2 Trim any remaining triangle points as needed and add the 2" x 12" rectangles and then the 2" x 14" rectangles as shown. Press the seam allowances toward the rectangles and trim the runner top to measure 15" wide.

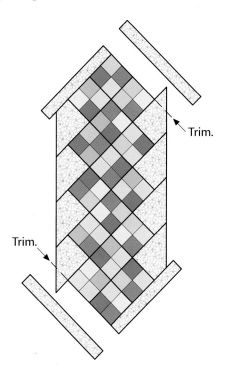

Finishing

Go to ShopMartingale.com/HowtoQuilt if you need more information on any of the finishing steps.

1 Layer, baste, and quilt your table runner.

2 Using the blue-stripe 2¼"-wide strips, prepare and attach the binding.

Square Tumble

A clever, contemporary way to set a table for four is with two table runners, using the runners for the place settings. The runners don't have to be identical, but they should be similar. The runners shown are created from two different, random layouts of the same block designs. These are simple to make, and the larger pieces in the runners will showcase your favorite accent fabrics.

FINISHED RUNNERS: 15½" x 93½"
FINISHED BLOCK: 15" x 15"
Designed and made by Natalie Barnes; quilted by Angela Walters

Materials

Materials are for 2 runners. Yardage is based on 42"-wide fabric. Fat quarters are 18" x 21".

8 to 10 fat quarters of assorted light prints for blocks
3 fat quarters of accent prints #1–#3 for block rectangles
1 fat quarter of accent print #4 for block squares and sashing strips
1 yard of light print for binding
2¾ yards of fabric for backing
2 pieces, 21" x 99", of batting

Cutting

From the 8 to 10 assorted light prints, cut a *total* of:
240 squares, 3½" x 3½"

From *each* of accent prints #1–#3, cut:
4 rectangles, 3½" x 15½" (12 total)

From accent print #4, cut:
3 strips, 3½" x 18"; crosscut into 12 squares,
   3½" x 3½"
6 strips, 1½" x 18"; crosscut into 6 strips, 1½" x 15½"

From the light print for binding, cut:
12 strips, 2¼" x 42"

Making the Blocks

1. Randomly select five assorted light 3½" squares and sew them together to make a strip measuring 3½" x 15½". Press the seam allowances in one direction. Make 36.

Make 36.

2. Randomly select four assorted light 3½" squares and sew them together with one accent #4 square as shown to make a strip measuring 3½" x 15½". Press the seam allowances in one direction. Make 12.

Make 12.

3. Arrange and sew three units from step 1, one unit from step 2, and one accent 3½" x 15½" rectangle as shown. Make eight of block A, two of block B, and two of block C.

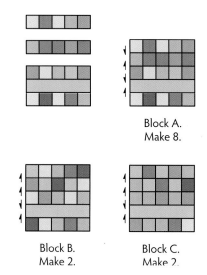

Block A.
Make 8.

Block B.
Make 2.

Block C.
Make 2.

● PRESSING POINTER

   If you want a specific fabric to stand out from the other fabrics in your block, press your seam allowances toward that piece to give it more dimension.

Assembling the Runners

1. Referring to the assembly diagrams on page 135, arrange the six blocks and three of the accent 1½" x 15½" strips on your design wall. Move the strips around and rotate the blocks until you are pleased with your layout and there is variation in the placement of the fabrics.

2. Remove the pieces from your design wall and stack them top to bottom, in the order in which you will sew them. As a precaution, place a pin through the blocks before carrying them to your machine. Sew the blocks and accent strips together. Press the seam allowances in one direction.

⬤ DOWNSIZED RUNNERS

To make two shorter table runners, cut half as many pieces as directed in the cutting list and make half as many blocks. Use three blocks in each runner and one accent strip. You'll have two runners that are 15½" x 46½". You could also cut the same number of pieces, make the 12 blocks, and use three blocks in each runner—you'll be making four shorter table runners at once!

Another option is to make a total of eight blocks. Use four blocks and two accent strips in each runner to make two runners that measure 15½" x 62½". Of course, you can always make just one runner using any number of blocks and accent strips that work well for your table.

3 Repeat steps 1 and 2 to assemble the second table runner.

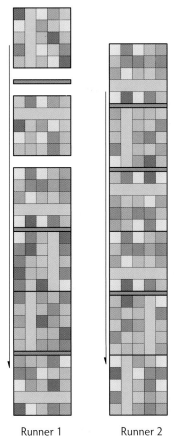

Runner 1   Runner 2

Quilt assembly

Finishing

Go to ShopMartingale.com/HowtoQuilt if you need more information on any of the finishing steps.

1 Layer, baste, and quilt your table runners.

2 Using the light 2¼"-wide strips, prepare and attach the binding.

Starry Night

Although piecing diamonds and setting in triangles can be challenging, Karen Soltys steadily navigates the way to piece one of her favorite blocks on point. East meets West as scraps of hand-dyed fabrics combine with an Asian indigo. Karen muses, "While the stars are reminiscent of Amish patchwork, they take on a whole new light against the Japanese print of the setting triangles."

FINISHED RUNNER: 15" x 69"
Designed and made by Karen Costello Soltys

Materials
Yardage is based on 42"-wide fabric.

½ yard of indigo print for setting triangles and end borders

Scraps of 10 assorted blue, red, brown, and olive solids (approximately 9" x 22" total of each color) for blocks

½ yard of red solid or hand-dyed fabric for binding

1 yard of fabric for backing

19" x 73" piece of batting

Cutting

For the Blocks

Select 3 of the assorted solids for each block—2 for the star points and 1 for the background. You can use the same fabric more than once in different positions if desired.

From *each* of the solids for the star points, cut:
1 strip, 2½" x 20" (10 total)

From *each* of the solids for the 5 block backgrounds, cut:
4 squares, 3½" x 3½" (20 total)
1 square, 5¼" x 5¼" (5 total); cut into quarters diagonally to yield 20 triangles

For the Remaining Pieces

From the indigo print, cut:
2 squares, 16" x 16"; cut each square into quarters diagonally to yield 8 triangles
4 strips, 1½" x 14"

From the red solid or hand-dyed fabric, cut:
5 strips, 2" x 42"

Making the Blocks

1 From each of the assorted solid 2½" x 20" strips, cut four 45° diamonds, 2½" wide.

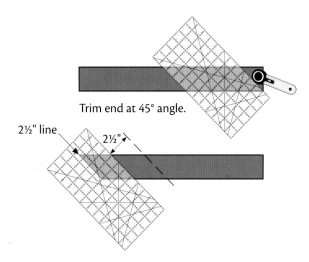

Trim end at 45° angle.

2½" line

2½"

2 Using the four diamonds from each of two different-colored fabrics, sew one diamond of each color together to make four pairs, starting and stopping stitching ¼" from the points.

Start and stop stitching ¼" from each end of seam.

Make 4 pairs for each block.

● SIMPLE SETUP FOR SET-IN SEAMS

Here's a tip to make set-in seams easy to manage. Just start and stop sewing ¼" from the points to leave the seam allowances free for stitching to the next piece in the block. You can use either a small ruler or a template to measure the distance, and then mark the starting and stopping points with a pencil. Or, perhaps you have a patchwork presser foot with ¼" markings that will make the work a cinch.

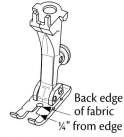

Back edge of fabric

¼" from edge

Notched presser foot

3 Sew one edge of a 3½" background square to one diamond point, starting ¼" from the inner point and sewing to the end. Remove the units from your machine and align the adjacent side of the square with the next diamond point. Again, start stitching ¼" from the inner point and sew to the end. Repeat with the remaining pairs.

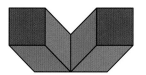

Set in square.

4 Sew the pairs of star points together to make two half blocks, starting ¼" from the inner point and sewing to the end.

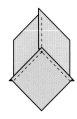

Make 2.

5 Sew a background triangle between the joined star points. Start ¼" from the inner point (the black dot on the illustration) and sew to the ends.

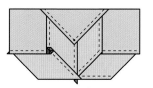

Set in triangle.

6 Sew the two half stars together, matching the inner points, and then sew the remaining two background triangles between the star points to complete the block.

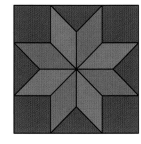

Join star halves.

Set in 2 remaining triangles to complete block.

7 Repeat steps 2–6 to make a total of five Eight-Pointed Star blocks. Press well, and then square up the blocks to measure 10".

Assembling the Runner

1 Arrange the blocks on point on your design wall or the floor in the order you'd like. Lay the indigo setting triangles between them.

2 Sew the blocks and triangles together in diagonal rows. Start sewing by aligning the square corner of the triangles with the corners of the blocks. The triangles are cut oversized to let the stars float in the background, which means the triangle points will extend well beyond the ends of the blocks.

3 Sew the rows together, matching seam intersections.

4 Using the indigo 1½"-wide strips, align one end of a strip with the block at one end of the table runner. Stitch the strip to the block and the setting-triangle extension. Press, and then trim the end of the strip at a 45° angle to align with the setting triangle. Repeat for both sides of both ends.

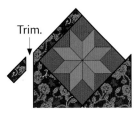 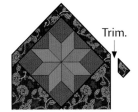

Trim. ← → Trim.

Finishing

Go to ShopMartingale.com/HowtoQuilt if you need more information on any of the finishing steps.

1 Layer, baste, and quilt your table runner.

2 Using the red or hand-dyed 2"-wide strips, prepare and attach the binding.

Winter Whimsy

Invite a bit of whimsy to your Christmas table! This simple, cheerful runner looks great on its own or as a backdrop for other seasonal decorations. Add a bowl of scented pinecones for a primitive, country look.

FINISHED RUNNER: 14" x 45"
Designed and made by Jeanne Large

Materials

Yardage is based on 42"-wide cotton fabric and 54"-wide wool. All wool is presumed to be felted wool, which is wool that has been washed and dried by machine to shrink the fibers and prevent raveling. If you are purchasing unfelted wool off the bolt, purchase extra to allow for shrinkage. To felt wool, machine wash in warm water and dry on a medium setting.

Wool

½ yard of cream for background
10" x 16" piece of green for trees
5" x 13" piece of brown for tree trunks
4" x 7" piece of gold for stars
8" x 10" piece of red for hearts

Cotton

⅓ yard of green print for binding
1⅜ yards of fabric for backing

Additional Materials

Fusible web (optional)
13 red buttons in various diameters from ¼" to ¾"

Cutting

From the cream wool, cut:
1 piece, 14" x 45"

From the green cotton, cut:
4 strips, 2½" x 42"

Appliquéing the Runner

1. The appliqué patterns are on pages 142 and 143. Jeanne used fusible-web appliqué, but you can prepare the following number of shapes for your favorite method of appliqué from the wool colors indicated:
   - 2 each of A, B, C, and D from green
   - 2 tree trunks from brown
   - 2 stars from gold
   - 4 hearts from red

2 Arrange the appliqué pieces on the cream felted wool as shown. Appliqué the shapes in place.

Finishing

Go to ShopMartingale.com/HowtoQuilt if you need more information on finishing steps. This project is finished without batting or quilting, and a preshrunk flannel is used as backing. Combined with the felted wool, this gives the runner a very soft, supple texture.

1 Baste the runner top to the backing.

2 Using the green 2½"-wide strips, prepare and attach the binding.

3 Quilt as desired.

4 Sew the red buttons between the hearts as shown in the photo on page 140.

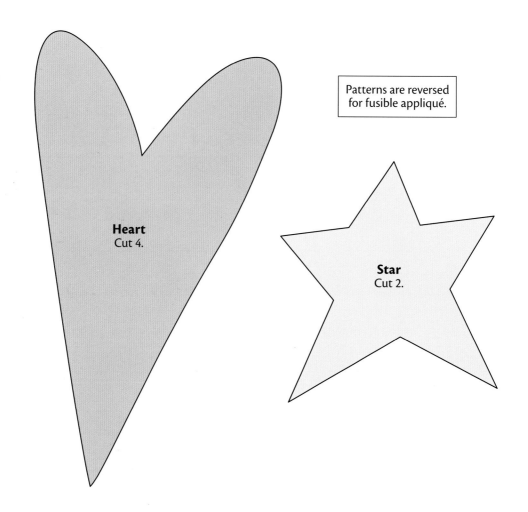

Patterns are reversed for fusible appliqué.

Heart
Cut 4.

Star
Cut 2.

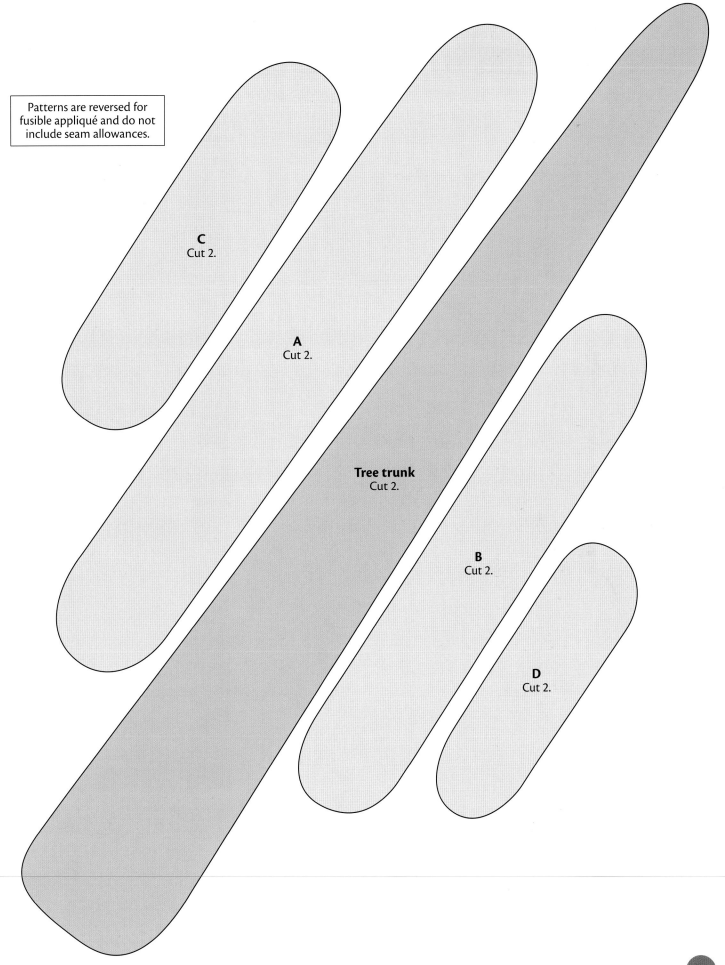

Patterns are reversed for fusible appliqué and do not include seam allowances.

C
Cut 2.

A
Cut 2.

Tree trunk
Cut 2.

B
Cut 2.

D
Cut 2.

Sunflower Duet

*"Kansas in late summer is full of sunflower fields,"
reports designer Lynne Hagmeier. "We cut them for
arranging, hang and dry them for the birds, and roast
the seeds for snacking." In this quilt, the sunflowers
reflect a wonderful glow in rich golds, browns, greens,
and rusts . . . and they couldn't be easier to grow.
Flower heads are Courthouse Steps blocks surrounded
by triangle squares in a look reminiscent of the classic
Kansas Troubles pattern.*

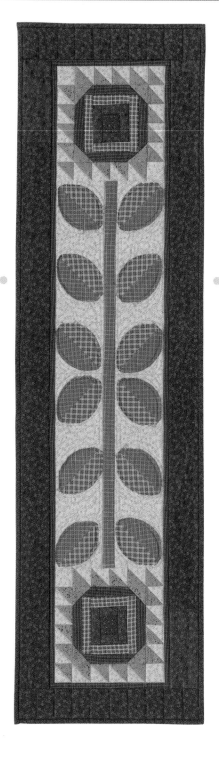

FINISHED RUNNER: 15½" x 54½"

Designed and made by Lynne Hagmeier; quilted by Nancy Arnoldy

Materials

*Yardage is based on 42"-wide
fabric. A fat quarter is 18" x 21"; fat
eighths are 9" x 21".*

⅝ yard of tan print for background

½ yard of brown small-scale print
for blocks and outer border

¼ yard of rust plaid for blocks and
inner border

¼ yard of dark green plaid flannel
for stem and leaves

1 fat quarter of gold print
for blocks

1 fat eighth of brown plaid
for blocks

1 fat eighth of medium green plaid
flannel for leaves

Scrap of dark brown mini-scale
print for blocks

⅓ yard of brown tone on tone for
binding

1¾ yards of fabric for backing

20" x 59" piece of batting

Freezer paper

● CUSTOMIZE THE FIT

To create a runner that will be
sized perfectly for your table,
simply add to or subtract
from the length of the stem
and the number of leaves and
background patches (half-
square triangles and spacers).

Cutting

**From the scrap of dark brown
mini-scale print, cut:**

2 squares, 2" x 2"

**From the brown small-scale
print, cut:**

1 strip, 1¼" x 42"; crosscut into:
  4 rectangles, 1¼" x 2"
  4 rectangles, 1¼" x 3½"

4 strips, 3" x 42"

From the brown plaid, cut:

4 rectangles, 1¼" x 3½"

4 rectangles, 1¼" x 5"

Continued on page 146

Continued from page 144

From the rust plaid, cut:
2 strips, 1¼" x 42"; crosscut into:
    4 rectangles, 1¼" x 5"
    4 rectangles, 1¼" x 6½"
3 strips, 1" x 42"

From the gold print, cut:
8 squares, 2" x 2"
18 squares, 2⅜" x 2⅜"

From the tan print, cut:
2 strips, 2⅜" x 42"; crosscut into 18 squares, 2⅜" x 2⅜"
2 strips, 2" x 42"; crosscut into:
    4 squares, 2" x 2"
    8 rectangles, 2" x 4½"
2 strips, 4⅞" x 42"; crosscut into 12 squares,
    4⅞" x 4⅞". Cut each square in half diagonally to
    yield 24 triangles.

From the dark green plaid flannel, cut:
1 strip, 1½" x 30½"

From the brown tone on tone, cut:
4 strips, 2½" x 42"

Making the Sunflower Blocks

The center portion of the Sunflower block is constructed in the same manner as the traditional Courthouse Steps. Finger-press the seam allowances away from the block center as you go.

1. Sew a brown small-scale print 1¼" x 2" rectangle to the top and bottom edges of a brown mini-print 2" square as shown; finger-press. Sew brown small-scale print 1¼" x 3½" rectangles to the sides of the unit; finger-press. Make two.

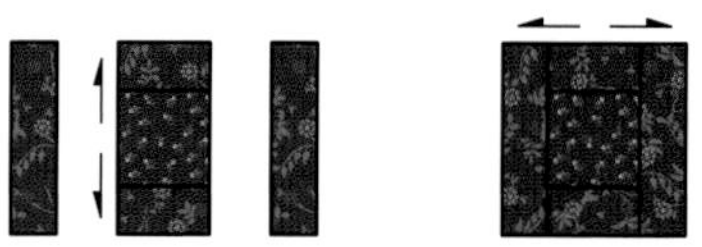

Make 2.

2. Use the method described in step 1 to sew the brown plaid 1¼" x 3½" and 1¼" x 5" rectangles to the units from step 1 as shown; finger-press. Sew the rust 1¼" x 5" and 1¼" x 6½" rectangles to the units; finger-press. Make two.

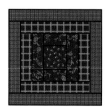

Make 2.

3. Use a pencil to draw a diagonal line on the wrong side of each gold 2" square. With right sides together and raw edges aligned, place a marked square on each corner of a unit from step 2 as shown. Stitch directly on the marked lines. Trim ¼" beyond the stitching line; press. Make two.

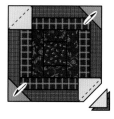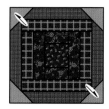

Make 2.

4. Use a pencil to draw a diagonal line on the wrong side of each tan 2⅜" square. With right sides together and raw edges aligned, place a marked square on a gold 2⅜" square; pin. Make 18. Stitch a scant ¼" from both sides of the line. Cut on the line to separate the sewn units; press. Make 36 half-square-triangle units.

Make 18.   Make 36.

5. Sew four units from step 4 together as shown; press. Make four of each.

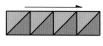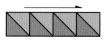

Make 4.   Make 4.

6 Arrange a unit from step 3, two of each unit from step 5, two half-square-triangle units, and two tan 2" squares as shown. Sew the units and squares into rows; press. Sew the rows together; press. Make two blocks.

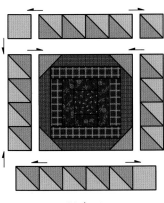

Make 2.

Making the Leaves

1 Use the half-leaf pattern on page 148 to make a template. Trace 12 leaves onto a piece of freezer paper and cut the leaves out directly on the traced lines.

2 With the waxy side down, press the freezer-paper half leaves onto the right side of the medium green flannel, with the long straight edge of the paper pattern on the bias of the fabric as shown. Cut out the leaves along the edge of the paper. Peel the freezer paper from the shapes and repeat to cut 12 half leaves from the remaining dark green flannel.

3 Position each half leaf on a tan half-square triangle, centering and aligning the straight edge of the leaf along the diagonal raw edge of the triangle as shown; pin. Make 12 of each.

Make 12 of each.

4 With right sides together, pin one medium green and one dark green flannel half-leaf unit from step 3 together along the diagonal edges; sew. Unfold and press the seam allowances open. Make 12. You will secure the raw edges after the layers of the runner are basted for quilting.

Make 12.

Assembling the Runner

Work on a large, flat surface such as a design wall, a table, or floor.

1 Arrange the pieced leaf squares, the tan 2" x 4½" rectangles, and the dark green 1½" x 30½" flannel strip as shown in the assembly diagram on page 148. Sew the leaf squares and rectangles together into rows; press. Sew the rows to the long sides of the dark green strip; press.

2 Sew a Sunflower block to each end of the unit from step 1, taking care to position the blocks as shown; press.

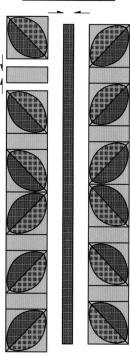

Assembly diagram

3 Sew the rust 1"-wide rust strips end to end with diagonal seams to make one long strip. Measure the length of the runner top through the center. Cut two inner-border strips to this measurement. Pin and sew one strip to each long side of the runner. Press the seam allowances toward the border.

4 Measure the width of the runner top through the center, including the borders. Repeat step 3 to trim, pin, and sew inner-border strips to the short ends of the runner; press.

5 Sew the brown small-scale print 3"-wide strips end to end with diagonal seams to make one long strip. Use the method described in steps 3 and 4 to measure, trim, pin, and sew the outer-border strips to the quilt. Press the seam allowances toward the newly added border.

Finishing

Go to ShopMartingale.com/HowtoQuilt if you need more information on any of the finishing steps.

1 Layer, baste, and quilt your table runner. Secure the leaves by straight stitching ¼" from the raw edges with green thread.

2 Using the brown tone-on-tone 2½"-wide strips, prepare and attach the binding.

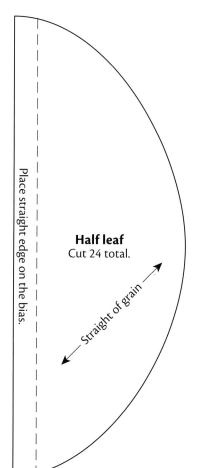

Straight edge of pattern includes seam allowance; curved edge is a cutting line.

Place straight edge on the bias.

Half leaf
Cut 24 total.

Straight of grain

Totally Taupe

A collection of Japanese taupe fabrics has a chance to shine in this easy table runner. The look here is serene and seasonless, perfect for any neutral-toned setting, but the design would be just as appealing in almost any fabric combination.

FINISHED RUNNER: 17" x 57" • **FINISHED BLOCK:** 4½" x 4½"
Designed and made by Mary V. Green; quilted by Krista Moser

Materials

Yardage is based on 42"-wide fabric.

1 yard *total* of assorted light and medium prints for block backgrounds and appliqués

½ yard *total* of assorted medium and dark prints for appliqués

½ yard *total* of medium prints for border

⅜ yard of dark print for binding

1⅛ yards of fabric for backing

23" x 62" piece of batting

Fusible web (optional)

● PRECUTS MAKE
● IT FAST!

You can easily make this table runner using precut 10" and 5" squares. With most of the cutting already done, you can get to the sewing faster!

Cutting

From the assorted light and medium prints, cut:

6 squares, 10" x 10"; cut each square in half diagonally to yield 12 triangles (6 will be extra)*

16 squares, 5" x 5"

From the medium prints for border, cut:**

2 strips, 2½" x 42"

2 strips, 2½" x 16"

2 strips, 2½" x 14"

From the dark print for binding, cut:

4 strips, 2" x 42"

*Mary used 6 different prints. If you prefer, cut 3 squares, cut each in half diagonally, and use both triangles from each square.

**If you use fat quarters, piece strips on the diagonal to get the length needed. For each end, you will need one 14"-long strip and one matching 16"-long strip.

Making the Blocks

The patterns for the circle appliqués are on page 153. Mary used fusible-web appliqué, but you can prepare the shapes for your favorite appliqué technique.

1. Prepare 16 circles using pattern A and the medium and dark prints. Prepare two half circles using pattern B and medium and dark prints. Prepare four half circles using pattern B and the light and medium prints.

2. Select a 5" background square for each circle. To center a circle on a background square, fold each square into quarters and lightly finger-press the folds. Fold the circle into quarters and lightly finger-press the folds. Unfold the pieces. Push a pin through the center point of the circle and into the center point of the square. Align the creases on the two pieces, remove the pin, and appliqué the circle to the square. Stitch around the edges of the appliqué by hand or machine using a blanket stitch or invisible machine stitch. Repeat to make 16 blocks.

3. Select a background triangle for each half-circle appliqué. To position a half circle on a triangle, fold it in half and lightly finger-press the fold. Fold the triangle in half and lightly finger-press. Handle these triangles carefully, as the long edge is on the bias and will stretch easily. Unfold the pieces and place the half circle on the triangle as shown, aligning the creases and the straight edges. Appliqué the shape to the triangle and stitch as before. Repeat to make six side triangles.

Make 16.　　　　Make 6.

Assembling the Runner

1. Referring to the assembly diagram below, arrange the blocks and setting triangles on a design wall, table, or floor. When you're pleased with the layout, sew each grouping of four 5" squares together to make a Four Patch block. Make four blocks.

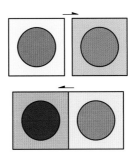
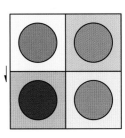

Make 4.

2. Sew the blocks and side triangles together in diagonal rows as shown. Press as indicated. Sew the rows together and press the seam allowances in one direction.

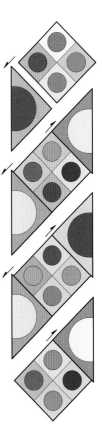

3 Use a rotary cutter and ruler to trim and even up the triangles along the long edges of the runner top, making sure to leave a ¼" seam allowance where they are joined to the Four Patch blocks.

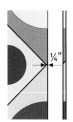

Adding the Border

1 Fold the 2½" x 42" border strips in half crosswise and finger-press the center point. Fold the runner top in half and finger-press the center point of the long edges. With right sides together and matching center points, pin and sew a border to each long edge of the runner. Press the seam allowances toward the borders. Trim the ends even with the edge of the runner top as shown.

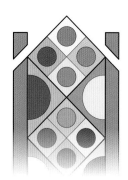

2 Sew a 2½" x 14" strip to the right edge of one pointed end of the runner; press. Trim the ends even with the runner top. Sew a matching 2½" x 16" strip to the left edge. Press and trim.

3 Repeat step 2 to sew the remaining strips to the opposite end of the runner top. Press and trim.

Finishing

Go to ShopMartingale.com/HowtoQuilt if you need more information on any of the finishing steps.

1 Layer, baste, and quilt your table runner.

2 Using the dark print 2"-wide strips, prepare and attach the binding.

Complement the circular shapes in your runner by quilting swooping curves.

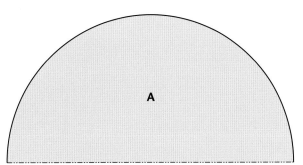

A

Flip along dashed line to complete pattern.

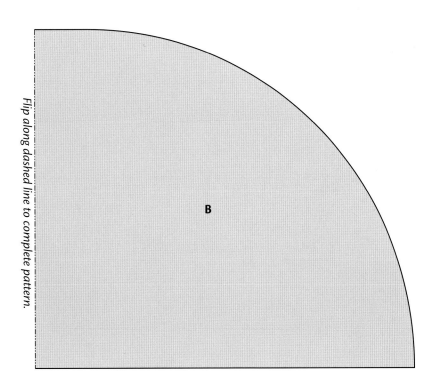

B

Flip along dashed line to complete pattern.

Patterns do not include
seam allowances.

Holly Jolly

Who could resist these adorable reindeer? The fabric with the white background gives the whole runner a burst of fun, and nothing adds whimsy—even at Christmastime!—quite like black-and-white polka dots.

FINISHED RUNNER: 12" x 40"
Designed and made by Linda Lum DeBono

Materials

Yardage is based on 42"-wide fabric. Fat quarters are 18" x 21".

1 fat quarter of green tree print for patchwork
1 fat quarter of green snowflake print for patchwork
1 fat quarter of green reindeer print for patchwork
1 fat quarter of red tree print for patchwork
1 fat quarter of red reindeer print for patchwork
1 fat quarter of red snowflake print for patchwork
1 fat quarter of white holiday print for patchwork
¼ yard of black-and-white print for patchwork
½ yard of fabric for backing

Cutting

From the green tree print, cut:
1 rectangle, 7½" x 12½"

From the green snowflake print, cut:
1 rectangle, 7½" x 12½"

From the green reindeer print, cut:
1 rectangle, 7½" x 12½"

From the red tree print, cut:
1 rectangle, 4½" x 12½"

From the red reindeer print, cut:
1 rectangle, 4½" x 12½"

From the red snowflake print, cut:
1 rectangle, 4½" x 12½"

From the white holiday print, cut:
1 rectangle, 7½" x 12½"

From the black-and-white print, cut:
6 strips, 2½" x 12½"

From the backing fabric, cut:
1 rectangle, 12½" x 40½"

● EVERYTHING UPRIGHT

Be aware of directional prints as you cut the pieces. In the sample, all the prints are cut parallel to the 12½" edges. For a different look, cut the prints parallel to the shorter edges of each rectangle and arrange them with their tops toward the center of the runner.

Assembling and Finishing the Runner

1 Fold and press each black-and-white strip in half lengthwise with the wrong sides together.

2 Place a pressed strip along each long edge of all three red rectangles, right sides together and matching the raw edges; pin.

3 Sew the green-print and white-print rectangles to the red-print rectangles as shown, securing the black-and-white strips between the rectangles.

4 Press the seam allowances toward the red rectangles, pressing the black-and-white strips away from the red rectangles. Topstitch the red rectangles ¼" from each seam.

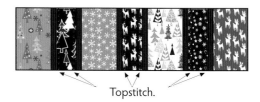

Topstitch.

5 With right sides together, sew the assembled runner front to the backing fabric. Leave a 5" opening for turning near the center of one long side. Clip the corners diagonally to reduce bulk and turn the runner right side out.

6 Gently work the corners into position, making sharp angles. Use a point turner or other tool to assist. Press the runner, turning the raw edges to the wrong side along the opening, and slip-stitch the opening closed.

7 Topstitch ¼" from the outer edges of the runner.

Glad Tidings

Angels announced the joyous news on the very first Christmas, and they endure as an uplifting holiday symbol. Made from whole cloth with no seams or piecing, this beautiful table runner features angel appliqués that stand out from the turquoise-sky background. A few metallic prints give the table runner a bit of Christmas sparkle.

FINISHED RUNNER: 14" x 40"
Designed and made by Cheryl Almgren Taylor

Materials

Yardage is based on 42"-wide fabric. A fat quarter is 18" x 21".

½ yard of turquoise print for background
⅜ yard of gold print for wing appliqués and binding
1 fat quarter of white print for angel appliqués
Scraps of peach, cream, honey yellow, and gold fabrics for appliqués
1⅓ yards of fabric for backing
18" x 44" piece of batting
Fusible web (optional)
Gold metallic thread for appliqué (optional)
Metallic needle (recommended)
Teflon pressing sheet (recommended)

Cutting

From the turquoise print, cut:
1 rectangle, 14" x 40"

From the gold print, cut:
3 strips, 2½" x 42"

Assembling the Runner

1 Using the patterns on pages 160 and 161, prepare the appliqué pieces for two angels. Cheryl used fusible-web appliqué, but you can use your preferred method. Consult the photo and materials list on this page for fabric choices as needed.

2 Center the prepared appliqué units 1½" from each end of the turquoise rectangle. Appliqué the angel units in place.

3 If desired, finish the raw edges of each appliqué piece using a machine blanket stitch, zigzag stitch, or satin stitch.

4 Use a pencil or fabric marker to make a mark 4" from each corner of the table-runner top. Draw a diagonal line connecting the points. Cut on the lines to angle the corners.

Finishing

Go to ShopMartingale.com/HowtoQuilt if you need more information on any of the finishing steps.

1 Layer, baste, and quilt your table runner.

2 Using the gold 2½"-wide strips, prepare and attach the binding.

● QUILTING THE RUNNER

Not sure what kind of quilting design to use? If you chose a print for the background fabric, consider quilting along its design lines as shown on page 158.

**Angel appliqué patterns
and placement guide, section A**

Patterns are reversed for
fusible appliqué and do not
include seam allowances.

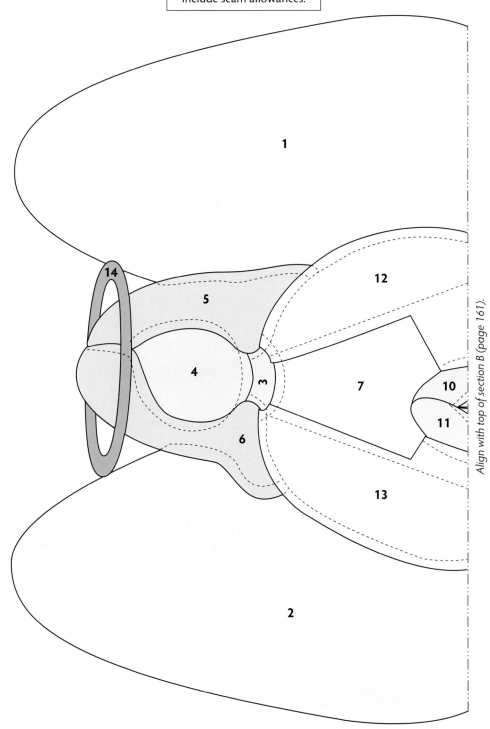

1

14

5

4

3

12

7

10

11

6

13

2

Align with top of section B (page 161).

Angel appliqué patterns
and placement guide, section B

Patterns are reversed for
fusible appliqué and do not
include seam allowances.

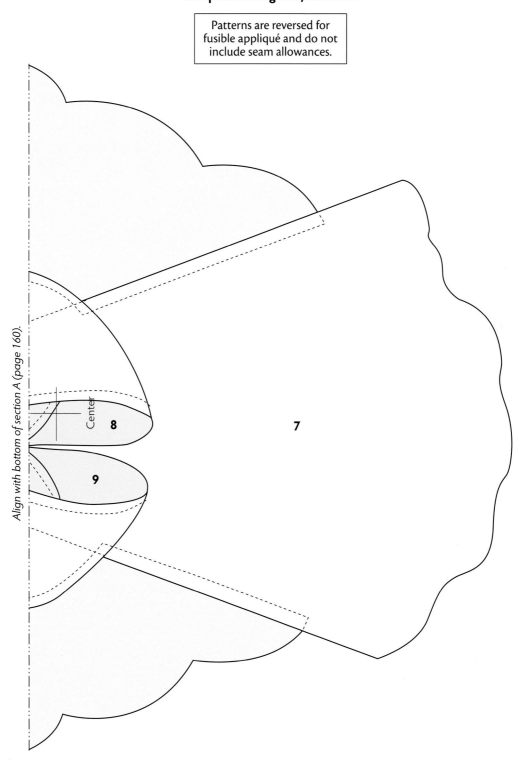

Align with bottom of section A (page 160).

Center

8

9

7

Table Toppers

Harvest Bouquet

This small quilt will fit the bill for anyone who loves both patchwork and appliqué. It has lots of pint-size charm and won't take long to make. It includes quilting cottons in fat eighths, fat quarters, and charm squares, plus luscious bits of wool for the appliqués. Who could ask for anything more?

FINISHED TOPPER: 22½" x 22½"
FINISHED BLOCK: 4" x 4"
Designed and made by Kim Diehl

Materials

Yardage is based on 42"-wide fabric. Fat quarters are 18" x 21"; charm squares are 5" x 5"; a fat eighth is 9" x 21".

Cotton

2 fat quarters of brown print for sashing strips and binding
1 fat quarter of tan print for blocks and sashing corner squares
1 fat quarter of orange print for border
9 charm squares of assorted prints for blocks
4 squares, 3½" x 3½", of assorted prints for border corner squares
1 fat eighth of dark green plaid for vines
¾ yard of fabric for backing

Wool

8 rectangles, 3" x 4", of assorted colors for tulip appliqués
8 squares, 2" x 2", of assorted colors for tulip-petal appliqués
Scraps of assorted greens for leaf appliqués

Additional Materials

27" x 27" piece of batting
Fusible web (optional)
¼" bias bar
Liquid fabric glue
#8 or #12 pearl cotton in a neutral color
Size 5 embroidery needle
Seam ripper

Cutting

From the tan print, cut:
9 squares, 2⅞" x 2⅞"; cut each square in half diagonally to yield 18 triangles
18 squares, 1⅞" x 1⅞"; cut each square in half diagonally to yield 36 triangles
52 squares, 1½" x 1½"

From each of the assorted print charm squares, cut:*
1 square, 2⅞" x 2⅞" (9 total); cut each square in half diagonally to yield 18 triangles
2 squares, 1⅞" x 1⅞" (18 total); cut each square in half diagonally to yield 36 triangles

Keep the patchwork pieces separated by print to simplify the piecing process.

Continued on page 166

Continued from page 164

From 1 brown fat quarter, cut:
24 rectangles, 1½" x 4½"

From the 2ⁿᵈ brown fat quarter, cut:
5 strips, 2½" x 22"

From the orange print, cut:
4 rectangles, 3½" x 16½"

From the dark green plaid, cut *on the bias*:
8 rectangles, 1" x 8"

Making the Blocks

1. Select a set of matching patchwork pieces cut from one of the assorted print charm squares. Join a tan print 2⅞" triangle with an assorted print 2⅞" triangle, stitching along the long diagonal edges. Press the seam allowances toward the assorted print. Trim away the dog-ear points. Repeat to make two large half-square-triangle units.

2. Repeat step 1 using four tan 1⅞" triangles and four assorted print 1⅞" triangles to make four small half-square-triangle units.

3. Lay out two small half-square-triangle units and two tan 1½" squares as shown. Join the pieces in each horizontal row. Press the seam allowances toward the tan print. Join the rows. Press the seam allowances to one side. Repeat to make two pieced units.

Make 2.

4. Lay out two large half-square-triangle units and two units from step 3 as shown. Join the units in each horizontal row. Press the seam allowances toward the large half-square-triangle units. Join the rows. Press the seam allowances to one side.

5. Repeat steps 1–4 to make nine pieced blocks measuring 4½" square, including the seam allowances.

Assembling the Topper

1. Lay out four tan print 1½" squares and three brown 1½" x 4½" rectangles, alternating them as shown. Join the pieces. Press the seam allowances toward the brown print. Repeat to make four sashing rows.

Make 4.

2. Lay out four brown 1½" x 4½" rectangles and three pieced blocks, alternating them as shown. Join the pieces. Press the seam allowances toward the brown print. Repeat to make three block rows.

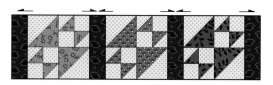

Make 3.

3. Referring to the photo on page 164, lay out the sashing rows and the block rows to form the table-topper center. Join the rows. Press the seam allowances toward the sashing rows.

4. Join orange 3½" x 16½" rectangles to opposite sides of the topper center. Press the seam allowances toward the orange print. Join an assorted print 3½" square to each end of the remaining orange 3½" x 16½" rectangles. Press the seam allowances toward the orange. Join these pieced rectangles to the remaining sides of the topper center. Press the seam allowances toward the orange. The topper should now measure 22½" square, including the seam allowances.

Preparing the Stems

1. With wrong sides together, fold each dark green plaid 1" x 8" rectangle in half lengthwise and use a scant ¼" seam allowance to stitch along the long raw edges to form a tube. Slide the bias bar through each tube to easily press it flat, centering the seam allowance so that it will be hidden from the front of the finished stem. (If the seam allowance will be visible, trim it to ⅛".)

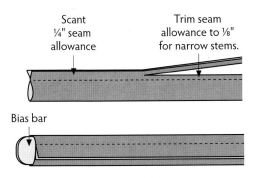

Scant ¼" seam allowance

Trim seam allowance to ⅛" for narrow stems.

Bias bar

2. Place small dots of liquid fabric glue along the seamline underneath the pressed seam allowance at approximately ½" to 1" intervals. Use a hot, dry iron on the wrong side of the stem to heat-set the glue and fuse the seams in place.

Preparing the Wool Appliqués

1. The appliqué patterns are on page 168. Kim used fusible-web appliqué, but you can prepare the following number of shapes for your favorite method of appliqué from the assorted felted wools:
   - 8 of pattern A
   - 24 of pattern B
   - 26 of pattern C

2. Cut out each freezer-paper shape approximately ¼" outside the drawn line; then cut away the center portion of the shape approximately ¼" inside the drawn lines (this will eliminate bulk and keep the appliqués soft and pliable after stitching). It isn't necessary to cut away the centers of the B shapes because of their small size.

3. Following the manufacturer's instructions, fuse a prepared A shape, paper side up, to each 3" x 4" rectangle of wool. Repeat with the prepared

B shapes, placing three B pieces onto each 2" square of wool. Fuse the prepared C shapes onto scraps of assorted green wool. Cut out each shape exactly on the drawn lines.

Stitching the Appliqués

1. Select a prepared A appliqué and a set of three matching B appliqués. Remove the paper backing from the B appliqués only. Place small dots of liquid fabric glue around the perimeter of each B piece and position them onto the A appliqué. Use a hot, dry iron to heat-set the glue and fuse the layers together from the front. Repeat with the remaining A and B appliqués.

● WOOL APPLIQUÉ MADE EASY

The combination of fusible adhesive and liquid glue produces ideal results because the iron-on adhesive finishes and stabilizes the underside of the wool edges to reduce fraying, while the glue-basted edges hold the layers of wool together beautifully for easy stitching without pinning.

2. Use pearl cotton and a size 5 embroidery needle to stitch the appliqués in place. Kim likes to stitch her appliqués using an overhand stitch or whipstitch rather than the traditional blanket stitch. Tie off and knot the threads from the back.

3. Referring to the table-topper photo, use a seam ripper to open a 1½"-wide area of two opposing corner blocks to insert the stems.

4. Remove the paper backing from all remaining appliqués. Using the photo as a guide, position four prepared tulip appliqués onto one corner of the table topper; pin in place. Lay out three prepared stems, tucking the raw ends into the open patchwork seam at least ¼" and curving them to join the tulips, again tucking under at least ¼". Trim away any excess stem length to achieve the look you desire. Place small dots of liquid glue underneath the stems at approximately ½" to 1" intervals to anchor them in place. Position and glue-baste a fourth stem

to connect the final tulip to the original portion of the design. Apply small dots of liquid fabric glue to the adhesive area of 14 leaves and position them along the stems as desired. Heat-set the appliqués and stems from the back of the table topper.

5 Use a needle and thread to hand stitch the patchwork opening, sewing along the original seamline.

6 Using a fine-gauge thread to match the dark green plaid and an appliqué needle, stitch the stems to the table topper. Use pearl cotton and a size 5 embroidery needle to stitch the wool appliqués in place.

7 Repeat steps 4–6 to complete the appliqué design on the opposite corner of the table topper.

Finishing

Go to ShopMartingale.com/HowtoQuilt if you need more information on any of the finishing steps.

1 Layer, baste, and quilt your table topper.

2 Using the brown-print 2½" x 22" strips, prepare and attach the binding.

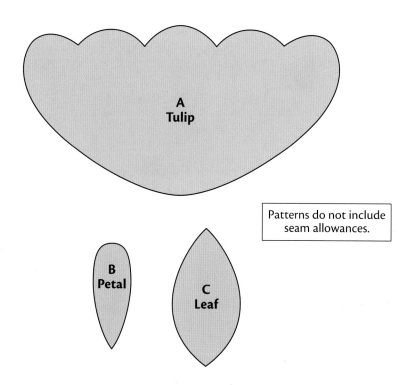

A
Tulip

Patterns do not include
seam allowances.

B
Petal

C
Leaf

Nothing but Pinwheels

This Pinwheel block, also known as Electric Fan, is interesting because it creates secondary pinwheels at the block intersections. Choose two colors for the blocks for two different-colored pinwheels as shown, or make the central pinwheels different colors and the secondary pinwheels a consistent color. Either way, the central pinwheels will be of one fabric, and the secondary pinwheels will have four different fabrics. Fun!

FINISHED TOPPER: 25½" x 30½"
FINISHED BLOCK: 5" x 5"
Designed and made by Ellen Pahl

Materials
Yardage is based on 42"-wide fabric. Charm squares are 5" x 5".

¾ yard of light print for blocks
30 charm squares OR ½ yard *total* of assorted brown prints for blocks
30 charm squares OR ½ yard *total* of assorted pink prints for blocks
¼ yard of brown print for binding
1 yard of fabric for backing
30" x 35" piece of batting

Cutting
From the light print, cut:
6 strips, 3¾" x 42"; crosscut into 60 squares, 3¾" x 3¾". Cut each square into quarters diagonally to yield 240 triangles.

From the brown prints, cut a *total* of:
30 squares, 3¾" x 3¾"; cut each square into quarters diagonally to yield 120 triangles

From the pink prints, cut a *total* of:
30 squares, 3¾" x 3¾"; cut each square into quarters diagonally to yield 120 triangles

From the brown print for binding, cut:
3 strips, 2⅛" x 42"

Making the Blocks

For each block, select eight light triangles, four matching brown print triangles, and four matching pink print triangles.

1 Sew a brown triangle to a light triangle along the short side as shown. Press. Make four. Repeat with the four pink triangles. For this block, always sew with either the brown or the pink triangle on top and the light print on the bottom.

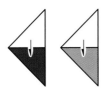

Make 4 of each.

2 Sew a pink unit to a brown unit. Make four quarter-square-triangle units. Press the seam allowances of two units toward the brown triangles and two units toward the pink triangles.

Make 2 of each.

3 Arrange the units as shown. Sew together in rows and press the seam allowances of both rows toward the brown. Sew the rows together and press to one side.

4 Repeat steps 1–3 to make a total of 30 blocks.

● **GOING UP OR DOWN?**

If you're using a directional print for the pink or brown triangles, arrange the units as you would like them to appear in the block before you sew.

Assembling the Topper

1 Arrange the blocks in six rows of five blocks each. Sew the blocks into rows and press the seam allowances in opposite directions from row to row.

2 Sew the rows together; press the seam allowances in one direction.

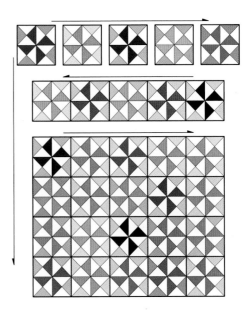

Finishing

Go to ShopMartingale.com/HowtoQuilt if you need more information on any of the finishing steps.

1 Layer, baste, and quilt your table topper.

2 Using the brown 2⅛"-wide strips, prepare and attach the binding.

May Baskets

Do you have a round table that needs dressing up? This little topper is the perfect centerpiece. Take advantage of the designer's simplified techniques, such as appliquéing the flower petals over a yellow square to make a detailed-looking flower, and adding buttons to the vines instead of appliquéing circles.

FINISHED TOPPER: 30½" x 30½"
Designed and made by Heather Mulder Peterson

Materials

Yardage is based on 42"-wide fabric.

⅞ yard of cream print for background
½ yard of green print for leaves and stems
⅛ yard *each* of 4 different colors for flowers
⅜ yard of brown print for baskets
Scrap of gold fabric for flower centers
½ yard of red stripe for binding
1 yard of fabric for backing
34" x 34" piece of batting
Fusible web (optional)
#5 black pearl cotton
16 red buttons, ⅝" diameter
8 red buttons, ½" diameter

Cutting

From the green print, cut:
2 strips, 3" x 42"; crosscut into 16 squares, 3" x 3"

From the cream print, cut:
1 square, 15½" x 15½"; cut into quarters diagonally to yield 4 triangles
1 square, 10½" x 10½"
8 squares, 5½" x 5½"
16 squares, 3" x 3"

From the brown print, cut:
3 strips, 3" x 42"; crosscut into:
    4 pieces, 3" x 10½"
    8 pieces, 3" x 5½"

From the red stripe, cut:
2½"-wide bias strips to total 115" in length

Making the Blocks

1 Draw a diagonal line from corner to corner on the wrong side of a green 3" square. Layer the marked square on one corner of a cream 5½" square, right sides together. Stitch directly on the marked line, and then trim ¼" from the stitching. Repeat to sew a green square to each cream 5½" square, pressing half of the seam allowances toward the green and half toward the cream so that the seams will nest when sewn together. Sew the units into pairs, pressing as indicated.

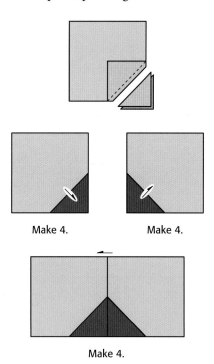

Make 4.   Make 4.

Make 4.

2 Repeat step 1 to sew two cream 3" squares to each brown 10½"-long piece, pressing as indicated.

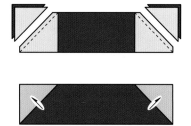

Make 4.

3 Repeat step 1 to sew a cream 3" square to the left side of a brown 5½"-long piece. Sew a green 3" square to the right side. Press as indicated. Make four of these units and four reverse. Sew the units into pairs; press.

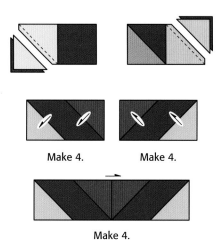

Make 4.   Make 4.

Make 4.

4 Sew the units from steps 1–3 together as shown to make four blocks. Square up each block to 10½" x 10½". Using the patterns on page 176, prepare the shapes for your favorite appliqué technique. Heather used fusible-web appliqué. Position and appliqué a basket handle and gold square to each block, referring to the photo on page 172 for placement. If desired, machine appliqué these shapes using a small zigzag stitch with matching thread. Next, position the petals and appliqué them in place. In the table topper shown, the petals were blanket-stitched with black topstitching thread.

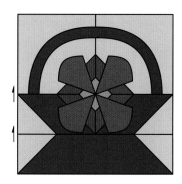

Make 4.

Assembling the Topper

1 Sew the blocks, the cream 10½" square, and the cream triangles into rows as shown, pressing the seam allowances away from the Basket blocks. Sew the rows together and press the seam allowances away from the center square.

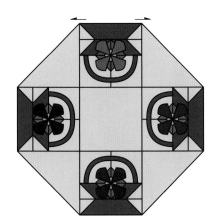

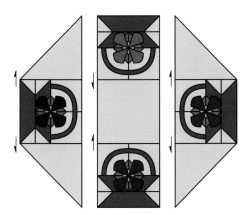

2 Appliqué the stems in place and then add leaves, referring to the photo for placement. Heather machine stitched these pieces using a small zigzag stitch with green thread.

Finishing

Go to ShopMartingale.com/HowtoQuilt if you need more information on any of the finishing steps.

1 Layer, baste, and quilt your table topper.

2 Using the red-stripe 2½"-wide strips, prepare and attach the bias binding.

3 Referring to the photo for placement, use the black pearl cotton to sew the red buttons along the vines.

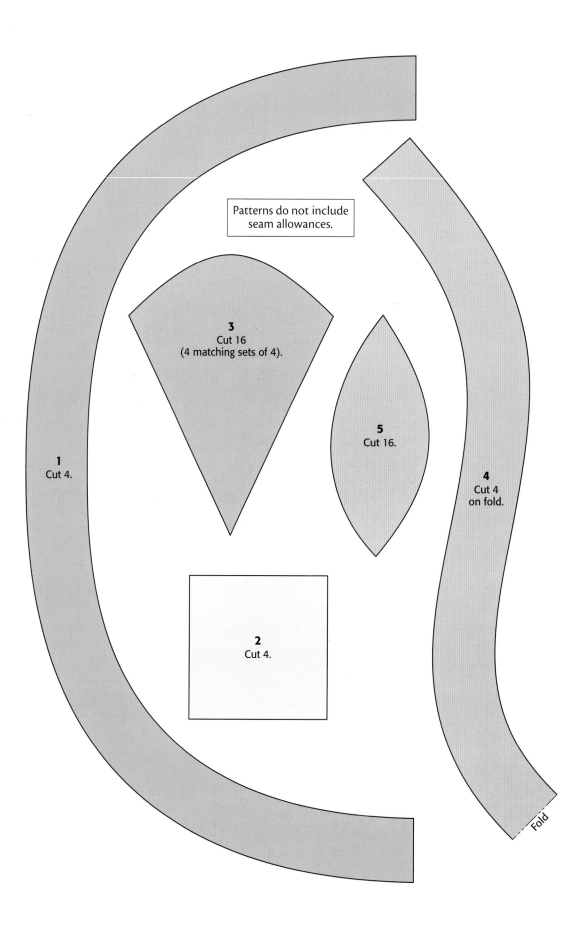

Patterns do not include seam allowances.

3
Cut 16
(4 matching sets of 4).

5
Cut 16.

1
Cut 4.

4
Cut 4
on fold.

2
Cut 4.

Fold

Xs and Os

This quilt started out as tic-tac-toe, but designer Ellen Pahl couldn't stop at nine blocks. Batiks are such fabulous fabrics that it's easy to keep going. Here's your chance to show off some of the batiks in your own collection. The X block is a standard Pinwheel, but with the "corners cut off." Pairing it with an O block adds up to extra fun.

FINISHED TOPPER: 20" x 20"
FINISHED BLOCK: 4" x 4"
Designed and made by Ellen Pahl

Materials

Yardage is based on 42"-wide fabric.

⅝ yard of light batik for blocks
4" x 6" piece *each* of 13 medium to dark batiks for x blocks
6" x 6" piece *each* of 12 medium batiks for O blocks
¼ yard of light plaid for binding*
¾ yard of fabric for backing
25" x 25" piece of batting

If you want to use a plaid cut on the bias, a fat quarter (18" x 21") will yield longer bias strips for fewer seams.

Cutting

From the light batik, cut:
2 strips, 2⅞" x 42"; crosscut into 26 squares, 2⅞" x 2⅞". Cut each square in half diagonally to yield 52 triangles.
5 strips, 1⅝" x 42"; crosscut into 100 squares, 1⅝" x 1⅝"
1 strip, 1¾" x 42"; crosscut into 12 squares, 1¾" x 1¾"

From *each* 4" x 6" batik piece, cut:
2 squares, 2⅞" x 2⅞"; cut each square in half diagonally to yield 4 triangles (52 total)

From *each* 6" x 6" batik piece, cut:
2 rectangles, 1¾" x 1⅞" (24 total)
2 rectangles, 1⅞" x 4½" (24 total)

From the light plaid, cut:
2⅛"-wide bias strips to total 94" in length

Making the X Blocks

1 Sew a medium or dark batik 2⅞" triangle to a light batik 2⅞" triangle along the long edges to make a half-square-triangle unit. Press. Make four identical units.

Make 4.

2 Sew the four units together as shown to make a Pinwheel block.

3 Draw a line diagonally on the wrong side of four light batik 1⅝" squares. Position a square on each corner of the Pinwheel block as shown and sew on the drawn lines. Trim the extra fabric to leave a ¼" seam allowance and press outward.

4 Repeat steps 1–3 to make a total of 13 X blocks.

Making the O Blocks

1 Sew matching medium batik 1¾" x 1⅞" rectangles to opposite sides of a light batik 1¾" square. Press the seam allowances away from the light square.

2 Sew matching medium batik 1⅞" x 4½" rectangles to the top and bottom of the unit from step 1. Press the seam allowances toward the center.

3 Draw a line diagonally on the wrong side of four light batik 1⅝" squares. Position a square on each corner of the block and sew on the drawn line. Trim the extra fabric to leave a ¼" seam allowance and press inward.

4 Repeat steps 1–3 to make a total of 12 O blocks.

Assembling the Topper

Arrange the X and O blocks in five rows of five blocks each, alternating them as shown in the assembly diagram. Sew the blocks into rows and press the seam allowances in opposite directions from row to row. Sew the rows together; press the seam allowances in one direction.

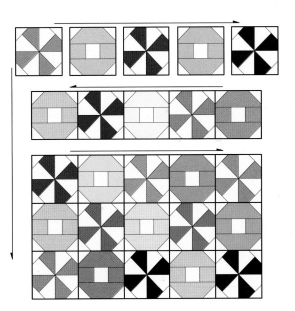

Finishing

Go to ShopMartingale.com/HowtoQuilt if you need more information on any of the finishing steps.

1 Layer, baste, and quilt your table topper.

2 Using the light plaid 2⅛"-wide strips, prepare and attach the bias binding.

Hourglass Charms

There are several ways to make triangle squares, also known as half-square-triangle units. The method employed in this quilt makes the most of the 5" charm squares. There's more than one route to success!

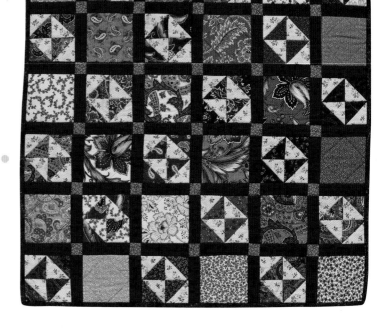

FINISHED TOPPER: 29" x 29"
FINISHED BLOCK: 4" x 4"
Designed and made by Mary Etherington and Connie Tesene

Materials

Yardage is based on 42"-wide fabric. Charm squares are 5" x 5".

38 charm squares of assorted medium-light to dark prints for blocks
⅓ yard of light print for block background
⅓ yard of dark brown print for sashing
⅛ yard of salmon print for cornerstones
¼ yard of dark brown print for binding
1 yard of fabric for backing
33" x 33" piece of batting

● STILL CHARMING

If you don't have a set of precut charm squares, you'll need a 5" x 10" piece *each* of at least nine dark prints, nine medium prints, and one light print. Cut each of the nine dark prints into two squares, 5" x 5". Cut each of the medium prints into two squares, 4½" x 4½", and cut the light print into two squares, 5" x 5".

Cutting

Select the two lightest charm squares to be used as background squares in two of the blocks. Separate the remaining 36 squares into two stacks: 18 medium and 18 dark squares.

From *each* of the 18 medium charm squares, cut:
1 square, 4½" x 4½" (18 total)

From the light print, cut:
2 strips, 5" x 42"; cut into 16 squares, 5" x 5"

From the dark brown print for sashing, cut:
7 strips, 1½" x 42"; cut into 60 strips, 1½" x 4½"

From the salmon print, cut:
1 strip, 1½" x 42"; cut into 25 squares, 1½" x 1½"

From the dark brown print for binding, cut:
3 strips, 1½" x 42"*

*If you don't have a 42" width of usable fabric, you may need 4 strips.

Assembling the Topper

1 Pair each of the 18 dark charm squares right sides together with a light background 5" square. (Remember, two of the background squares will be from your charm pack and a little different than your other background squares.)

2 Cut each dark/light pair into quarters that measure 2½" x 2½". Keep squares of the same fabrics together.

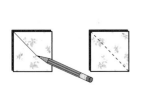

3 With the light fabric on top, mark a diagonal line from corner to corner on the paired 2½" squares. Stitch along the line. Trim so there's a ¼" seam allowance. Press seam allowances toward the dark fabric. Make four matching triangle squares.

Discard.

Make 4.

4 Combine the four matching triangle squares into a block as shown; press.

Make 18.

5 Repeat steps 3 and 4 to complete 18 blocks.

6 Arrange the blocks, alternating with the medium-value 4½" squares, in six rows of six blocks each. Place a 1½" x 4½" sashing strip between each to make a block row. Alternate six 4½" sashing strips with 1½" cornerstones as shown to make a sashing row. Sew into rows, and then sew the rows together. Press as shown.

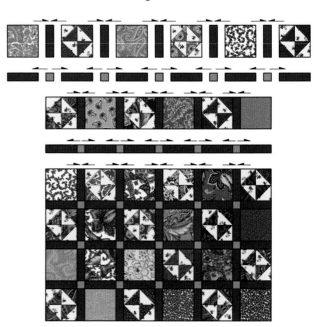

Finishing

Go to ShopMartingale.com/HowtoQuilt if you need more information on any of the finishing steps.

1 Layer, baste, and quilt your table topper.

2 Using the dark brown 1½"-wide strips, prepare and attach the binding. (Mary and Connie used single-fold binding, not double-fold.)

Christmas Glow

Heather proudly proclaims that she loves Christmas quilts and believes every home needs a few! Versatile pieces make it easy to spread cheer from room to room. This quilt, for example, can be used as a table topper, or you can cut a hole in the center and use it as a tree skirt.

FINISHED TOPPER: 46½" at the widest point
Designed and made by Heather Mulder Peterson

Materials

Yardage is based on 42"-wide fabric. A fat quarter is 18" x 21".

1⅛ yards of red print for checkerboards, holly berries, outer borders, and binding

½ yard of gold print for star points and candle flames

½ yard of purple print for star background

⅓ yard of cream print for checkerboards and candles

⅓ yard of black solid for holly blocks

1 fat quarter of black print for candle blocks

¼ yard of green print for holly leaves and candleholders

3 yards of fabric for backing

51" x 51" piece of batting

Fusible web (optional)

Cutting

From the red print, cut:
8 strips, 2¼" x 42"; crosscut into:
   3 pieces, 2¼" x 18"
   4 pieces, 2¼" x 14"
   4 pieces, 2¼" x 12"
   4 pieces, 2¼" x 11"
   4 pieces, 2¼" x 9¼"
   4 pieces, 2¼" x 7½"
5 strips, 2½" x 42"

From the cream print, cut:
3 strips, 2¼" x 42"; crosscut into:
   4 pieces, 2¼" x 18"
   3 pieces, 2¼" x 11"

From the gold print, cut:
2 strips, 6⅝" x 42"; crosscut into 8 squares, 6⅝" x 6⅝"

From the purple print, cut:
4 rectangles, 7½" x 12¾"

From the green print, cut:
4 squares, 4" x 4"

From the black print, cut:
4 squares, 7½" x 7½"

From the black solid, cut:
2 squares, 9½" x 9½"

Making the Blocks

1. Sew the red print and cream print 11"-long strips together along the long edges as shown, pressing the seam allowances toward the red. Cut this strip set into four segments, 2¼" wide.

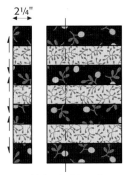

Make 1 strip set.
Cut 4 segments.

2. Sew the red print and cream print 18"-long strips together along the long edges as shown, pressing the seam allowances toward the red. Cut this strip set into seven segments, 2¼" wide.

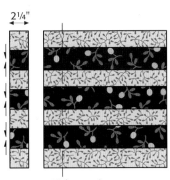

Make 1 strip set.
Cut 7 segments.

3. Sew the segments from step 1 and three segments from step 2 together as shown and square up the block to 12¾" x 12¾".

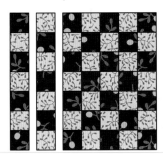

Make 1.

4. Draw a diagonal line from corner to corner on the wrong side of the gold squares. Layer a marked square on one corner of each purple rectangle, right sides together. Stitch directly on the marked line, and then trim ¼" from the stitching. Repeat to sew a marked gold square to the other end of each purple rectangle. Press the seam allowances toward the gold. Sew one of the remaining strip-set segments from step 2 to each block as shown and press toward the red-and-cream segments.

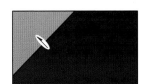

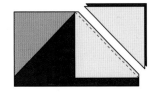
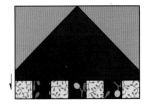

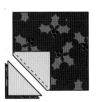

Make 4.

5. Repeat step 4 to sew a green square to a corner of each black print square. Press the seam allowances toward the green.

Make 4.

6 With the triangle at the lower left, sew a red-print 7½" strip to the left side of each block, pressing the seam allowances toward the red. Sew a red-print 9¼" strip to the bottom of the block and press the seam allowances toward the red.

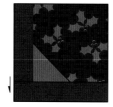

Make 4.

7 Draw a diagonal line on each of the black-solid 9½" squares. Sew ⅛" from both sides of the line and cut on the drawn line. (This is done to help stabilize the bias edge while the block is machine appliquéd.) Sew a red-print 12" strip to the left side of each triangle as shown and press the seam allowances toward the red. Sew a red-print 14" strip to the other side, press the seam allowances toward the red, and trim the strips even with the bottom of the triangle.

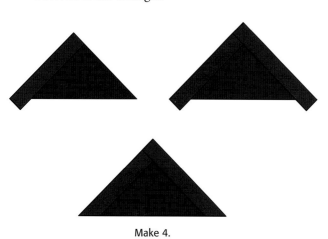

Make 4.

8 Using the patterns on page 187, prepare the shapes for your favorite appliqué technique. Appliqué the shapes to the blocks from steps 6 and 7 as shown in the photo on page 183. Heather used fusible-web appliqué, then she machine appliquéd the flame and candle using a small zigzag stitch in matching thread, and appliquéd everything else using a blanket stitch with black topstitching thread.

Assembling the Topper

1 Lay out the checkerboard block, the blocks from step 4 of the preceding section, and the appliquéd candle blocks as shown. Sew the blocks into rows, pressing the seam allowances as indicated. Sew the rows together and press as directed.

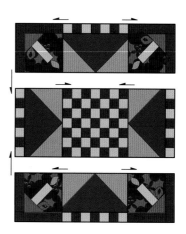

2 Add the triangle units, pressing the seam allowances as directed.

Finishing

Go to ShopMartingale.com/HowtoQuilt if you need more information on any of the finishing steps.

1 Layer, baste, and quilt your table topper.

2 Using the red-print 2½"-wide strips, prepare and attach the binding.

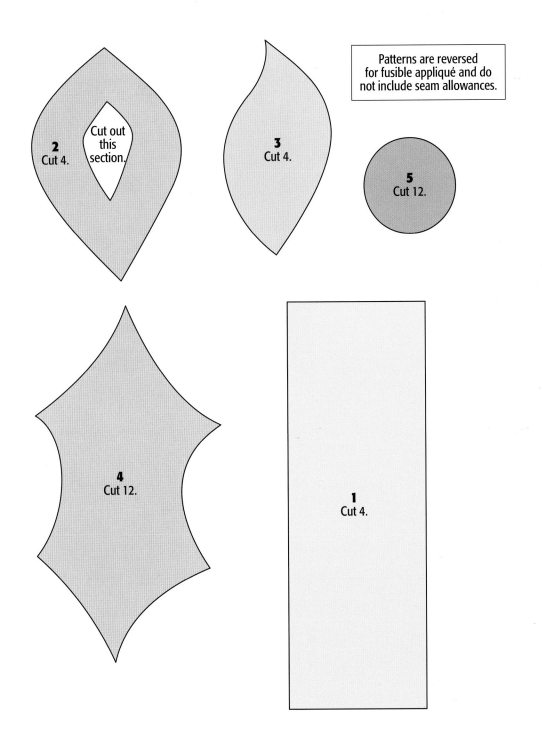

Patterns are reversed for fusible appliqué and do not include seam allowances.

2 Cut 4.

Cut out this section.

3 Cut 4.

5 Cut 12.

4 Cut 12.

1 Cut 4.

Chocolate-Covered Churn Dashes

Stepping out of one's fabric "comfort zone" is not always easy, but designer Cheryl Wall likes to challenge herself. Although pink fabrics are not regular players in her quilts, she loved the old-fashioned look of these prints. Combining them with brown fabrics reminded her of a box of cherry-filled chocolates. Chocolate and quilting—now that's a comfort zone!

FINISHED TOPPER: 42½" x 42½"
FINISHED BLOCK: 6" x 6"

Designed and made by Cheryl Wall; quilted by Jeanne Preto

Materials

Yardage is based on 42"-wide fabric.

1 yard *total* of assorted pink prints for blocks

1 yard *total* of assorted brown prints for blocks and middle border

⅞ yard of pink floral for inner and outer borders

⅝ yard *total* of assorted cream prints for blocks

½ yard of brown print for binding

3 yards of fabric for backing

51" x 51" piece of batting

Cutting

From the assorted pink prints, cut a *total* of:

116 squares, 2½" x 2½"
116 rectangles, 1½" x 2½"

From the assorted cream prints, cut a *total* of:

60 squares, 2½" x 2½"
48 rectangles, 1½" x 2½"
24 squares, 1½" x 1½"

From the assorted brown prints, cut a *total* of:

4 strips, 2½" x 30½"
65 squares, 2½" x 2½"
60 rectangles, 1½" x 2½"
24 squares, 1½" x 1½"

From the pink floral, cut:

8 strips, 2½" x 30½"
20 squares, 2½" x 2½"
8 rectangles, 1½" x 2½"

From the brown print for binding, cut:

5 strips, 2¼" x 42"

Making the Blocks

Block 1

1 Draw a diagonal line on the wrong side of four matching pink 2½" squares. With right sides together, place each marked square on a cream 2½" square and sew on the drawn line. Trim away the excess fabric on one side, leaving a ¼" seam allowance. Make four pink/cream half-square-triangle units. Press.

Make 4.

2 Sew a brown rectangle and a pink rectangle of the same print used in step 1 together lengthwise. Press the seam allowances toward the brown rectangle. Make four matching units.

3 Lay out one matching brown 2½" square with the units from steps 1 and 2 in three rows as shown. Sew the pieces together in rows, and then sew the rows together to complete the block. Do not press the seam allowances yet. Make one block.

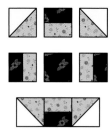

Block 1.
Make 1.

Block 2

1 Pair a brown 2½" square with a pink 2½" square; sew the pair together as in block 1, step 1. Repeat to make two matching brown/pink half-square-triangle units. Pair two cream 2½" squares with two pink 2½" squares to make two matching cream/pink half-square-triangle units.

2 Draw a diagonal line on the wrong side of two cream 1½" squares. With right sides together, position a marked square on one end of a brown 1½" x 2½" rectangle. Stitch on the marked line and trim ¼" from the stitching. Repeat to add the second marked cream square to the other end of the rectangle. Sew the flying-geese unit to a pink rectangle as shown in the block diagram.

3 Sew a cream rectangle and a pink rectangle together lengthwise. Press the seam allowances toward the pink rectangle. Make three.

4 Lay out one cream 2½" square and the pieces from steps 1, 2, and 3 in three rows as shown. Sew the pieces together in rows, and then sew the rows together to complete the block. Do not press the seam allowances. Make a total of four blocks.

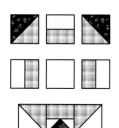

Block 2.
Make 4.

HINTS

- As you're sewing the individual blocks, try to press the seam allowances toward the darker fabrics in each block whenever possible.

- Because you will be rotating the blocks as you lay them out, you may find it easiest not to press the seam allowances until after the blocks are stitched together into rows. At that point, press the seam allowances in the first row in one direction. When joining the first and second rows, make sure the seam allowances in the second row go in the opposite direction of those in the first row so that they butt against each other. After sewing the rows together, press the seam allowances in the same direction as they were stitched. Continue in this manner until all of the rows are joined and pressed.

Block 3

1 Pair a brown 2½" square with a pink 2½" square; sew the pair together as in block 1, step 1. Repeat to make two matching brown/pink half-square-triangle units. Pair two cream 2½" squares with two pink 2½" squares to make two matching cream/pink half-square-triangle units.

2 Sew one brown 1½" square to one end of a cream 1½" x 2½" rectangle as shown. Trim the excess fabric leaving a ¼" seam allowance and press. Repeat, sewing a brown square to one end of another cream rectangle as shown; press. Sew each unit to a pink rectangle as shown; press.

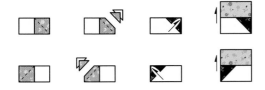

3 Sew a brown rectangle and a pink rectangle together lengthwise. Press the seam allowances toward the brown rectangle. Make two.

4 Lay out one brown 2½" square and the pieces from steps 1, 2, and 3 in three rows as shown. Sew the pieces together in rows, and then sew the rows together to complete the block. Do not press the seam allowances. Make a total of four blocks.

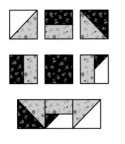

Block 3.
Make 4.

Block 4

1 Pair a brown 2½" square with a pink 2½" square; sew the pair together to make a brown/pink half-square-triangle unit. Make two. Pair two cream 2½" squares with two pink 2½" squares to make two cream/pink half-square-triangle units.

2 Make one flying-geese unit using one 1½" x 2½" cream rectangle and two 1½" brown squares. Sew the unit to a pink rectangle as shown in the block diagram. Press the seam allowances toward the pink rectangle.

3 Sew a brown rectangle and a pink rectangle together lengthwise. Press the seam allowances toward the brown rectangle. Make three.

4 Lay out one brown 2½" square and the pieces from steps 1, 2, and 3 in three rows as shown. Sew the pieces together in rows, and then sew the rows together to complete the block. Do not press the seam allowances. Make a total of four blocks.

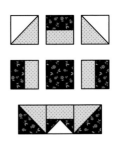
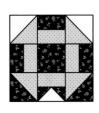

Block 4.
Make 4.

Block 5

1 Pair a brown 2½" square with a pink 2½" square; sew the pair together to make a brown/pink half-square-triangle unit. Make two. Pair two cream 2½" squares with two pink 2½" squares to make two cream/pink half-square-triangle units.

2 In the same manner as before, sew a 1½" cream square to one end of a brown rectangle as shown; trim and press. Sew a second cream square to one end of another brown rectangle as shown; trim and press. Sew each unit to a pink rectangle as shown; press.

3 Sew a cream 1½" x 2½" rectangle and a pink rectangle together lengthwise. Press the seam allowance toward the pink rectangle. Make two.

4 Lay out one cream 2½" square and the pieces from steps 1, 2, and 3 in three rows as shown. Sew the pieces together in rows, and then sew the rows together to complete the block. Do not press the seam allowances. Make a total of eight blocks.

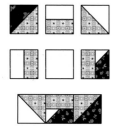
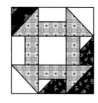

Block 5.
Make 8.

Block 6

1 Pair a brown 2½" square with a pink 2½" square; sew the pair together to make a brown/pink half-square-triangle unit. Make two. Pair one cream 2½" square with one pink 2½" square to make one cream/pink half-square-triangle unit. Pair one floral 2½" square with one pink 2½" square to make one floral/pink half-square-triangle unit.

2 In the same manner as before, sew a brown 1½" square to one end of a cream rectangle; trim and press. Sew a second brown square to one end of another cream rectangle as shown; trim and press. Sew each unit to a pink rectangle as shown; press.

3 Sew a brown rectangle and a pink rectangle together lengthwise. Press the seam allowances toward the brown rectangle. Make two.

4 Lay out one brown 2½" square and the pieces from steps 1, 2, and 3 in three rows as shown. Sew the pieces together in rows, and then sew the rows together to complete the block. Do not press the seam allowances. Make a total of four blocks.

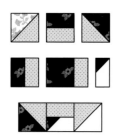

Block 6.
Make 4.

Block 7

1 Pair a floral 2½" square with a pink 2½" square; sew the pair together to make a floral/pink half-square-triangle unit. Make four.

2 Sew a brown rectangle and a pink rectangle together lengthwise. Sew a floral rectangle and a pink rectangle together lengthwise. Press the seam allowances toward the pink rectangles. Make two of each.

3 Lay out one brown 2½" square and the pieces from steps 1 and 2 in three rows as shown. Sew the pieces together in rows, and then sew the rows together to complete the block. Do not press the seam allowances. Make a total of four blocks. Set these blocks aside for the border.

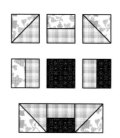
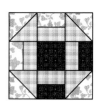

Block 7.
Make 4.

Assembling the Topper

1 Arrange blocks 1–6 in five rows as shown so that the block backgrounds form the secondary Barn Raising pattern.

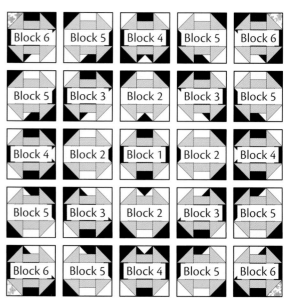

Quilt layout

2 Sew the blocks together in rows. Press the seam allowances in opposite directions from row to row. Sew the rows together, and press the seam allowances in one direction. The table topper should measure 30½" square.

3 Sew floral 2½"-wide strips to both long edges of a brown 2½"-wide strip. Press the seam allowances toward the brown strip. Repeat to make four border strips.

4 Sew border strips to the top and bottom of the table topper. Press the seam allowances toward the border.

5 Sew a block 7 to each end of the two remaining border strips as shown below. Press the seam allowances toward the border strips, and then sew the borders to the sides of the topper, matching the seam intersections. Press the seam allowances toward the border.

Finishing

Go to ShopMartingale.com/HowtoQuilt if you need more information on any of the finishing steps.

1 Layer, baste, and quilt your table topper.

2 Using the brown 2¼"-wide strips, prepare and attach the binding.

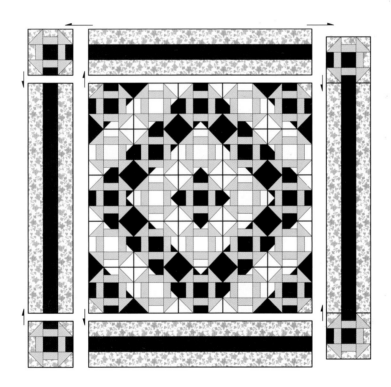

Checkerberry Bliss

All roads lead to bliss as you fashion rows of gently furrowed Four Patch blocks, and then surround them with baskets of blossoms and berries ripe for the picking. Set against a backdrop of soft midnight sky, these garden glories will forever be in bloom.

FINISHED TOPPER: 60½" x 60½"
FINISHED BLOCK: 6" x 6"
Designed by Kim Diehl

Materials

Yardage is based on 42"-wide fabric. Fat eighths are 9" x 21"; chubby sixteenths are 9" x 10½".

2⅞ yards of black print for blocks, border, appliqués, and binding

1⅝ yards of green print for blocks, border, and appliqués

⅞ yard of cream print for blocks and appliqués

½ yard of muted gold print for appliqués

½ yard of dark green print for vines and appliqués

1 fat eighth *each* of brown and coordinating green print for appliqués

7 chubby sixteenths *total* of assorted muted red, pink, lavender, blue, and orange prints for appliqués

4 yards of fabric for backing

67" x 67" piece of batting

Fusible web (optional)

⅜" bias bar

Cutting

Appliqué patterns A–F are on page 199. Kim uses freezer-paper appliqué and machine stitching, but you can prepare the shapes for your favorite method. For more details on appliqué, go to ShopMartingale.com/HowtoQuilt for free information, or see Kim's book Simple Appliqué *(Martingale, 2015) for a variety of appliqué techniques.*

From the green print for blocks, cut:

9 strips, 3½" x 42"; crosscut into 98 squares, 3½" x 3½"

1 strip, 9½" x 42"; crosscut into 4 squares, 9½" x 9½"

Reserve the remaining scraps for the leaf appliqués.

From the dark green print, cut on the *bias* grain:

12 rectangles, 1¼" x 2½"

16 rectangles, 1¼" x 4½"

8 strips, 1¼" x 18"

8 strips, 1¼" x 15"

From the remaining green prints, cut a *total* of:

64 using a random mix of patterns E and E reversed

From the cream print, cut:

10 strips, 2" x 42"

88 using pattern F

From the black print, cut on the *lengthwise* grain:

4 strips, 9½" x 42½"

Continued on page 196

Continued from page 194

From the remaining black print, cut:
10 strips, 2" x 42"
7 strips, 2½" x 42"
12 using pattern B

From the brown print, cut:
4 using pattern A

From the muted gold print, cut:
28 using pattern C

From *each* of the 7 assorted muted red, pink, lavender, blue, and orange prints, cut:
4 using pattern D (total of 28)

Making the Blocks

Sew all pieces with right sides together unless otherwise noted.

1 Sew each cream 2" x 42" strip to a black 2" x 42" strip along one long edge to make a strip set. Press the seam allowances toward the black. Repeat for a total of 10 strip sets. Crosscut the strip sets into 196 segments, 2" wide.

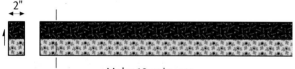

2"

Make 10 strip sets.
Cut 196 segments.

2 Join two strip-set segments as shown to make a four-patch unit. Press the seam allowance to one side. Repeat for a total of 98 four-patch units measuring 3½" square, including the seam allowances. *Note:* Take care that all of the four-patch units are assembled with the pieces consistently positioned as shown; this will help ensure that your finished table-topper center duplicates the pattern of the featured project.

Make 98.

3 Lay out two four-patch units and two green 3½" squares. Join the pieces in each horizontal row. Press the seam allowances toward the green. Join the rows. Press the seam allowances to one side. Repeat for a total of 49 Four Patch Variation blocks measuring 6½" square, including the seam allowances.

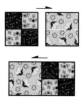

Make 49.

Assembling the Topper

1 Lay out seven Four Patch Variation blocks, turning every other block to position the center seam allowances in opposing directions. Join the blocks. Press the seam allowances in one direction. Repeat for a total of seven pieced rows.

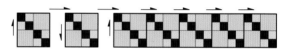

Make 7.

2 Lay out the pieced rows, turning every other row to position the seam allowances in opposing directions. Join the rows. Press the seam allowances in one direction. The pieced table-topper center should now measure 42½" square.

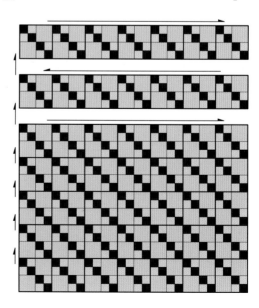

Appliquéing the Border Strips

1 With right sides together, fold a black 9½" x 42½" strip in half crosswise and lightly press a center crease.

Center crease

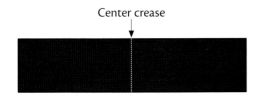

2 With wrong sides together, fold each dark green 1¼"-wide bias segment in half lengthwise and use a scant ¼" seam allowance to stitch along the long raw edges to form a tube. Slide the bias bar through each tube to easily press it flat, centering the seam allowance so that it will be hidden from the front of the finished seam. (If the seam allowance will be visible, trim it to ⅛".)

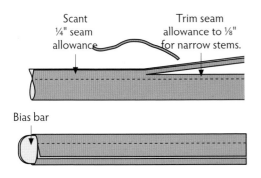

Scant ¼" seam allowance

Trim seam allowance to ⅛" for narrow stems.

Bias bar

3 Place small dots of liquid fabric glue along the seamline underneath the pressed seam allowance at approximately ½" to 1" intervals. Use a hot, dry iron on the wrong side of the stem to heat-set the glue and fuse the seam allowances in place.

4 Fold a prepared A appliqué in half and finger-press a center crease. Align the creases of the appliqué and the black border strip to center the vase, positioning the bottom of the vase approximately 1¼" up from the bottom border edge. Pin in place.

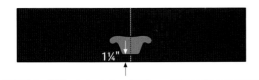

1¼"

5 Referring to the illustration, lay out the vines on the border strip, ensuring that all raw ends are overlapped well where they intersect and join the vase. When you are pleased with their positions, remove the vase and appliqué the vines in place.

● DUPLICATING APPLIQUÉD BORDERS

Here's a quick trick for easily duplicating the design of appliquéd borders with a repeated design. Lay out, baste, and stitch your first border as desired. Next, lay the completed border strip on a carpeted area, smooth away any wrinkles, and lay the next strip to be appliquéd exactly over the top of the original piece. Use a water-soluble marker to gently trace along the raised edge of the vines and stems positioned below the top piece. This traced design will serve as a blueprint to duplicate the placement of the vines and stems, and once they are in place, filling in with the remaining appliqués is a snap.

6 Reposition the vase and appliqué it in place.

7 Using the photo on page 194 as a guide, work from the bottom layer to the top to position and secure the B, C, D, E, E reversed, and F appliqués. Please note that for the featured table topper, the E and E reversed appliqués were randomly positioned without regard to their direction and the pointed leaf ends were also randomly placed up or down for added interest.

8 Repeat steps 4–7 for a total of four appliquéd border strips.

Adding the Border

1 Join appliquéd border strips to the right and left sides of the table-topper center. Carefully press the seam allowances toward the border strips, taking care not to apply heat to the appliqués.

2 Join a green 9½" square to each end of the remaining appliquéd border strips. Carefully press the seam allowances toward the black. Join these pieced strips to the remaining sides of the topper center. Carefully press the seam allowances toward the borders. The finished table topper should measure 60½" square, including the seam allowances.

Finishing

Go to ShopMartingale.com/HowtoQuilt if you need more information on any of the finishing steps.

1 Layer, baste, and quilt your table topper.

2 Using the black 2½" x 42" strips, prepare and attach the binding.

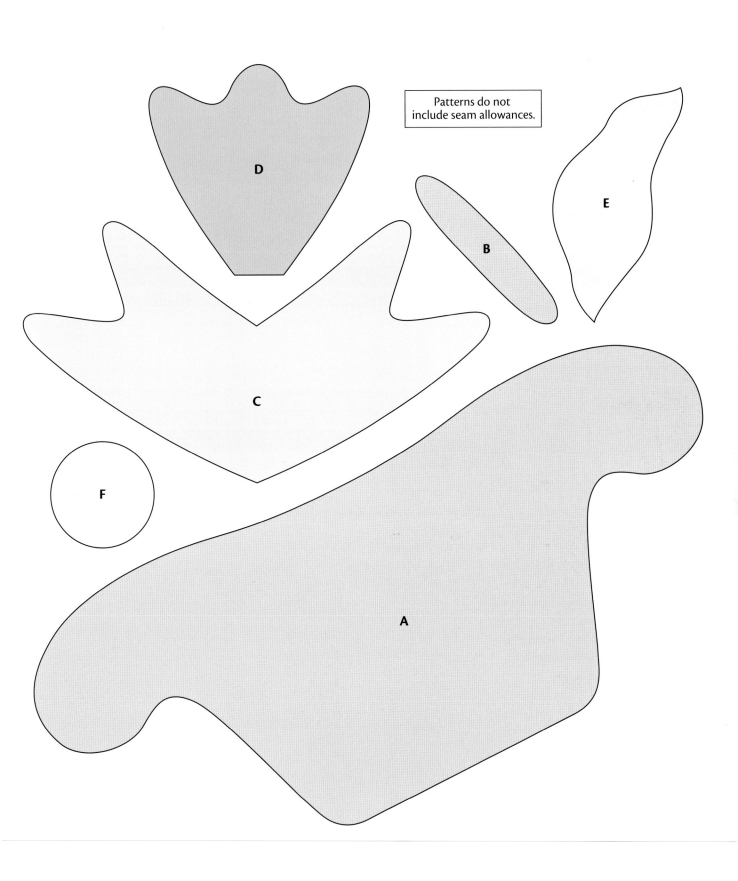

Patterns do not include seam allowances.

D

B

E

C

F

A

It's not hard to say good-bye to summer when you have the warm, inviting hues of fall at your fingertips. Autumn-themed appliqués and patchwork hint at the simple pleasures of the season—pumpkins for picking, leaves crunching underfoot, and glorious colors to behold.

FINISHED TOPPER: 48½" x 48½"

Designed and made by Heather Mulder Peterson

Materials

Yardage is based on 42"-wide fabric.

2 yards *total* of assorted prints for blocks and outer border

1 yard of black plaid for blocks and binding

¾ yard of cream print for appliqué background

⅜ yard of black fabric for inner border

Assorted scraps in orange, green, gold, and brown for appliqués

3 yards of fabric for backing

52" x 52" piece of batting

Fusible web (optional)

Cutting

From the assorted prints, cut:

16 rectangles, 2" x 8"
16 rectangles, 2" x 6½"
16 rectangles, 2" x 5"
16 rectangles, 2" x 3½"
16 squares, 2" x 2"
40 squares, 4½" x 4½"

From the cream print, cut:

10 strips, 2" x 42"; crosscut into:
16 rectangles, 2" x 8"
16 rectangles, 2" x 6½"
16 rectangles, 2" x 5"
16 rectangles, 2" x 3½"
16 squares, 2" x 2"

From the black plaid, cut:

5 strips, 2" x 42"; crosscut into 96 squares, 2" x 2"

4 squares, 4½" x 4½"

2½"-wide bias strips to total 210" in length

From the black border fabric, cut:

4 strips, 2½" x 42"

Making the Blocks

1 Sew a print 2" square, a cream 2" square, and two black-plaid 2" squares into a four-patch unit. Press the seam allowances away from the black plaid. Sew a cream 3½" rectangle to the right side and a print 3½" rectangle to the left side, pressing the seam allowances toward these rectangles.

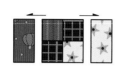

2 Sew a black-plaid 2" square to one end of a print 5" rectangle and sew this unit to the top of the block. Repeat with another black-plaid 2" square and a cream 5" rectangle and sew this unit to the bottom of the block so that the black squares form a diagonal line. Press the seam allowances toward the strips at the top and bottom. Sew a cream 6½" rectangle to the right side and a print 6½" rectangle to the left side, pressing the seam allowances toward these rectangles.

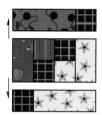

3 Sew a black-plaid 2" square to one end of a print 8" rectangle and sew this unit to the top of the block. Repeat with another black-plaid 2" square and a cream 8" rectangle and sew this unit to the bottom of the block, pressing the seam allowances toward these pieces. Square up each block to 9½" x 9½".

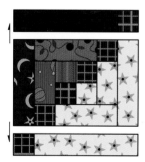

Make 16.

Assembling the Topper

1 Sew the blocks into four sections of four blocks each. Square up each section to 18½" x 18½".

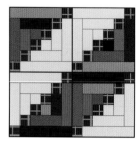
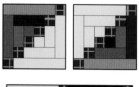

Make 4.

2 Using the patterns on pages 204 and 205, prepare the shapes for your favorite appliqué technique. Heather used fusible-web appliqué.

3 Appliqué the oak leaf and acorn shapes to the large cream area of each table-topper section, referring to the photo on page 200 and the diagram below for placement. If desired, machine appliqué the shapes using a blanket stitch with black topstitching thread.

4 Sew all four sections together as shown and square up the topper center to 36½" x 36½". Appliqué the pumpkin, stem, leaf, and vine appliqué shapes. You can also make the curlicue pumpkin stem by using a wide zigzag stitch.

5 Cut two of the black 2½"-wide strips to a length of 36½" each and sew them to the sides of the topper center. Cut the remaining two black strips to a length of 40½" (piecing if needed) and sew these strips to the top and bottom of the topper. Press the seam allowances toward the black borders. Square up the topper to 40½" x 40½".

6 Sew the print 4½" squares into four strips of 10 squares each. Press the seam allowances in one direction. Sew two of these strips to the sides of the table topper and press the seam allowances toward the black inner borders. Add the black plaid 4½" squares to the ends of the remaining two strips and press as directed by the arrows. Sew these strips to the top and bottom of the topper and press the seam allowances toward the black inner borders.

Finishing

Go to ShopMartingale.com/HowtoQuilt if you need more information on any of the finishing steps.

1 Layer, baste, and quilt your table topper.

2 Using the black-plaid 2½"-wide strips, prepare and attach the bias binding.

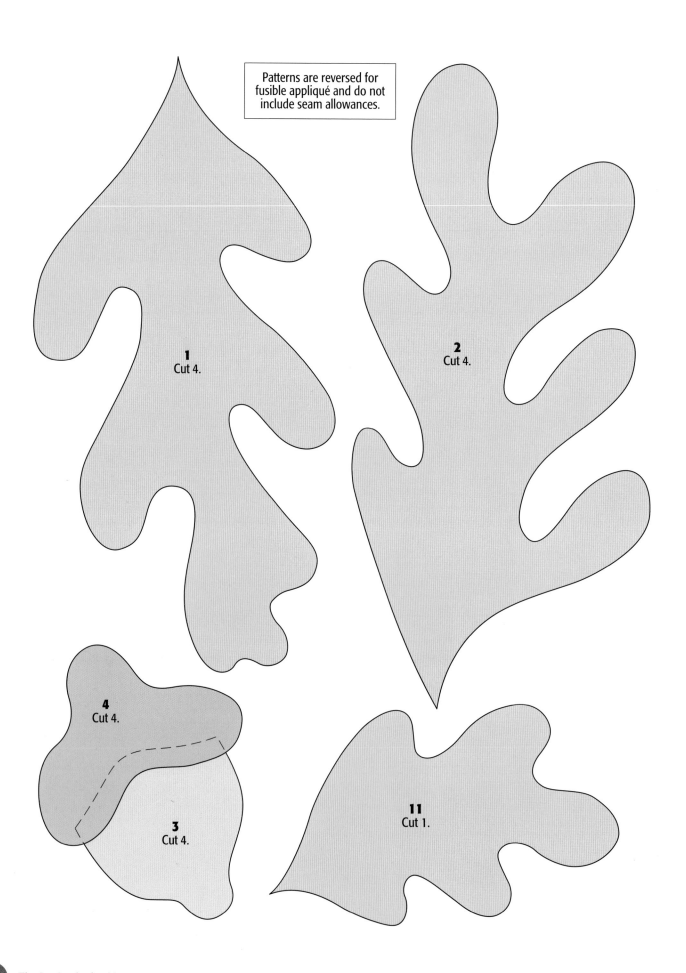

Patterns are reversed for fusible appliqué and do not include seam allowances.

1
Cut 4.

2
Cut 4.

4
Cut 4.

3
Cut 4.

11
Cut 1.

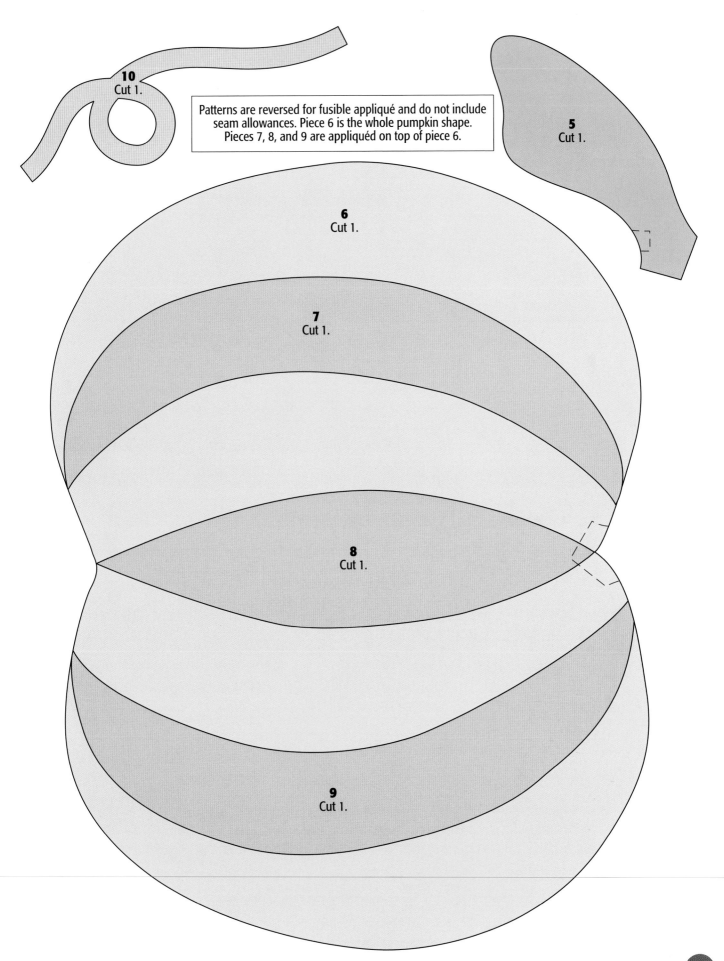

10
Cut 1.

Patterns are reversed for fusible appliqué and do not include seam allowances. Piece 6 is the whole pumpkin shape. Pieces 7, 8, and 9 are appliquéd on top of piece 6.

5
Cut 1.

6
Cut 1.

7
Cut 1.

8
Cut 1.

9
Cut 1.

Holly Berry

This small quilt is sure to brighten a holiday meal, whether it's topping a table or gracing the wall as a festive decoration. This is an easy design for beginning quilters because of the large, simple appliqué pieces.

FINISHED TOPPER: 42½" x 42½"
FINISHED BLOCK: 11¼" x 11¼"
Designed by Cheryl Almgren Taylor

Materials

Yardage is based on 42"-wide fabric.

1⅜ yards of red print for blocks, outer border, and binding

1⅛ yards of cream print for blocks and inner border

⅓ yard of dark green print 1 for sashing

¼ yard of gold print for sashing

¼ yard of dark green print 2 for holly leaf appliqués

Scraps of assorted red fabrics for berry appliqués

2⅞ yards of fabric for backing

47" x 47" piece of batting

Fusible web (optional)

Cutting

From the cream print, cut:
4 squares, 9" x 9"
4 strips, 6½" x 42"

From the red print, cut:
8 squares, 6½" x 6½"; cut each square in half diagonally to yield 16 triangles
5 strips, 2" x 42"
2½"-wide bias strips to total 180" in length

From dark green print 1, cut:
9 strips, 1" x 42"; cut 1 strip in half crosswise to yield 2 strips, 1" x 21" (1 will be extra)

From the gold print, cut:
5 strips, 1" x 42"; cut 1 strip in half crosswise to yield 2 strips, 1" x 21"

Making the Blocks

1 Using the patterns on page 209, prepare the holly and berry appliqués for your favorite method from the fabrics indicated.

2 Refer to the block placement guide to arrange the prepared appliqué pieces on the cream print squares in the order indicated. Appliqué the shapes in place.

Block placement guide

3 If desired, finish the raw edges of each appliqué piece using a blanket, zigzag, or satin stitch.

4 Trim each square to 8½" x 8½".

5 Sew a red triangle to each side of the appliquéd squares, adding opposite sides first. Press the seam allowances toward the triangles. Square up the blocks to 11¾" square.

Make 4.

Making the Sashing

1 Sew a dark green 1" x 42" strip to each long edge of a gold 1" x 42" strip to make strip set A. Repeat to make a total of four strip sets. Press the seam allowances toward the green strips. Crosscut the strip sets into 12 segments, 11¾" wide, and 9 segments, 1" wide.

Strip set A.
Make 4. Cut 12 segments, 11¾" wide,
and 9 segments, 1" wide.

2 Sew a gold 1" x 21" strip to each long edge of a dark green 1" x 21" strip to make strip set B. Press the seam allowances toward the green strip. Crosscut the strip set into 18 segments, 1" wide.

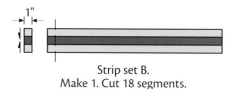

Strip set B.
Make 1. Cut 18 segments.

3 Join B segments to the sides of each 1"-wide A segment to make a nine-patch unit. Make a total of nine units.

Make 9.

Assembling the Topper

1 Join three 11¾" strip set A sashing segments and two blocks in alternating positions to make a block row. Press the seam allowances toward the sashing. Repeat to make a total of two rows.

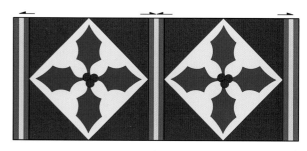

Make 2.

2 Join three nine-patch units and two sashing segments in alternating positions to make a sashing row. Press the seam allowances toward the sashing. Repeat to make a total of three rows.

Make 3.

3 Refer to the assembly diagram below to sew the sashing rows and block rows together. Press the seam allowances toward the sashing rows.

4 Measure the table topper for the borders. Use the cream 6½"-wide strips to add the inner border.

5 Refer to the corner and side placement guides at right to arrange the remaining prepared appliqué pieces on the border in the order indicated. Appliqué the shapes in place. If you wish, finish the raw edges of each appliqué piece using a blanket stitch, zigzag stitch, or satin stitch.

6 Join the red 2"-wide strips to the quilt top for the outer border.

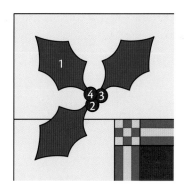

Corner placement guide

Side placement guide

Quilt assembly

Finishing

Go to ShopMartingale.com/HowtoQuilt if you need more information on any of the finishing steps.

1 Layer, baste, and quilt your table topper.

2 Using the red 2½"-wide strips, prepare and attach the bias binding.

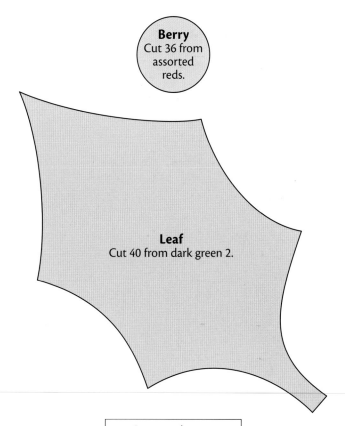

Berry
Cut 36 from assorted reds.

Leaf
Cut 40 from dark green 2.

Patterns do not include seam allowances.

Whirlwind

Most, although not all, of the fabrics in this quilt are Japanese, but designer Ellen Pahl says not to worry about mixing in another type of fabric. Sometimes the variety "makes things more interesting." The block used in this quilt has several names: Twin Sisters, Windmill, Water Wheel, Pinwheel, and Whirlwind.

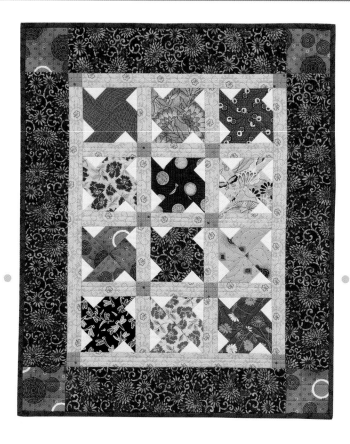

FINISHED TOPPER: 21" x 25½"
FINISHED BLOCK: 3½" x 3½"
Designed and made by Ellen Pahl

Materials

Yardage is based on 42"-wide fabric. A fat quarter is 18" x 21".

- 14" x 14" piece *each* of 12 assorted prints for blocks and outer-border corner squares
- ¼ yard of purple floral for outer border
- ¼ yard of light taupe print for sashing and inner border
- 1 fat quarter of white print for blocks
- 2" x 18" piece of dark taupe print for sashing and inner-border squares
- ¼ yard of dark print for binding
- ⅞ yard of fabric for backing
- 26" x 31" piece of batting
- Freezer paper *OR* half-square-triangle ruler

Cutting

From *each* of the assorted prints, cut *on the bias*:
1 strip, 2" x 18"*

From the white print, cut *on the bias*:
6 strips, 1¾" x 18"*

From the light taupe print, cut:
4 strips, 1½" x 42"; crosscut into:
   17 rectangles, 1½" x 4"
   2 strips, 1½" x 13"
   2 strips, 1½" x 17½"

From the dark taupe print, cut:
10 squares, 1½" x 1½"

From the purple floral, cut:
2 strips, 3½" x 19½"
2 strips, 3½" x 15"

From one of the assorted prints, cut:
4 squares, 3½" x 3½"

From the dark print for binding, cut:
3 strips, 2⅛" x 42"

*Cutting the strips on the bias will result in blocks with straight-grain edges.

Making the Blocks

1 Sew an assorted-print bias strip to each long edge of a white bias strip. Press.

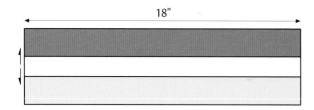

18"

2 If you are using freezer paper, trace the cutting guide pattern on page 213 onto the dull side of a piece of freezer paper at least eight times; cut out the freezer-paper templates. Press eight templates, shiny side down, to the strip set from step 1 as shown, aligning the dashed line on the template with the appropriate seam. Cut out four along the bottom edge and four along the top edge. If you are using a half-square-triangle ruler, align the dashed yellow line at the top of the ruler with the upper seamline. Cut eight triangles from the strip set, four along the top and four along the bottom.

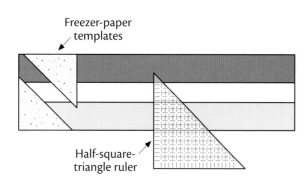

Freezer-paper templates

Half-square-triangle ruler

3 Gently remove the tiny triangle of the second fabric color from the point of each piece.

4 Sew each set of four matching units from step 2 together to make the blocks.

5 Repeat steps 1–4 to make a total of 12 blocks.

Assembling the Topper

1 Arrange the blocks in four horizontal rows of three blocks each, inserting the light taupe 1½" x 4" sashing strips between the blocks. Add the dark taupe sashing squares and sew the block rows and sashing rows as shown. Press. Sew the rows together and press.

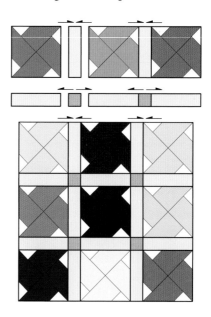

2 Add the light taupe 1½" x 17½" inner-border strips to the sides of the table topper. Press.

3 Sew a dark taupe 1½" corner square to each end of the light taupe 1½" x 13" inner-border strips. Press. Sew the strips to the top and bottom of the topper.

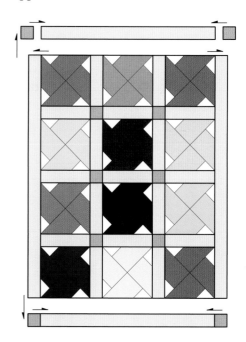

4 Sew the purple 3½" x 19½" outer-border strips to the sides of the topper. Press.

5 Sew a 3½" corner square to each end of the purple 3½" x 15" outer-border strips. Press. Sew the strips to the top and bottom of the topper.

Finishing

Go to ShopMartingale.com/HowtoQuilt if you need more information on any of the finishing steps.

1 Layer, baste, and quilt your table topper.

2 Using the dark 2⅛"-wide strips, prepare and attach the binding.

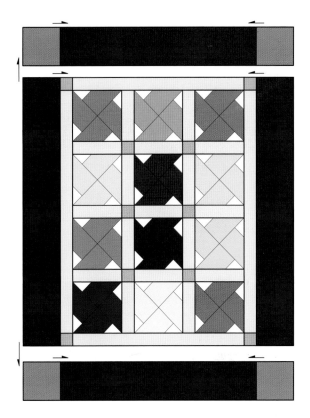

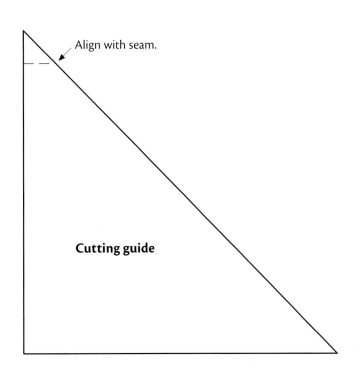

Align with seam.

Cutting guide

Mini Mountains

If you've ever doubted that a small project could have a mighty impact, this petite topper may change your mind. The small size makes it a perfect project for practicing your points, which can feel like a pretty mighty achievement in itself.

FINISHED TOPPER: 15" x 19" • **FINISHED BLOCK:** 3" x 3"
Designed and made by
Mary Etherington and Connie Tesene

Materials

Yardage is based on 42"-wide fabric. Charm squares are 5" x 5".

30 assorted medium to dark charm squares for blocks and pieced border
18 assorted light to medium charm squares for block backgrounds
¼ yard of pink print for side and corner setting triangles
¼ yard of brown print for binding
⅝ yard of fabric for backing
20" x 24" piece of batting

● MAKING DO

If you don't have charm squares, you'll need one fat eighth (9" x 21") *each* of nine medium to dark fabrics. Cut two 2⅞" squares and eleven 1⅞" squares from each fabric; you may need a couple of additional small squares for the border. You'll also need one fat eighth *each* of six light to medium fabrics for the backgrounds. Cut six 1⅞" squares and three 1½" squares from each fabric.

Cutting

From *each* of 18 medium to dark charm squares, cut:

1 square, 2⅞" x 2⅞" (18 total); cut each square in half diagonally to yield 36 triangles
3 squares, 1⅞" x 1⅞" (54 total); cut each square in half diagonally to yield 108 triangles

From the remaining 12 medium to dark charm squares, cut:

4 squares, 1⅞" x 1⅞" (48 total); cut each square in half diagonally to yield 96 triangles (4 will be extra)

From *each* of the light to medium charm squares, cut:

2 squares, 1⅞" x 1⅞" (36 total); cut each square in half diagonally to yield 72 triangles
1 square, 1½" x 1½" (18 total)

From the pink print, cut:

3 squares, 6" x 6"; cut each square into quarters diagonally to yield 12 triangles (2 are extra)
2 squares, 4½" x 4½"; cut each square in half diagonally to yield 4 triangles

From the brown print, cut:

2 strips, 2¼" x 42"

Making the Blocks

Each block is made from two medium/dark 2⅞"
triangles, four medium/dark 1⅞" triangles, four light/
medium 1⅞" triangles, and one light/medium 1½"
square. Many (but not all) of the blocks have the
same light/medium background fabric, an approach
that designers Mary and Connie believe helps the
individual blocks show more clearly.

1. Sew two different 2⅞" triangles together, being
   careful not to stretch the bias edges. Press the
   seam allowances in one direction. Repeat with
   the remaining 2⅞" triangles to make 18 half-
   square-triangle units.

Make 18.

2. Pair four matching light/medium 1⅞" triangles
   and four assorted medium/dark triangles. Sew
   the triangle pairs together and press the seam
   allowances in one direction. Make 72 half-
   square-triangle units for the blocks. Repeat
   with the remaining 1⅞" triangles to make
   approximately 64 additional units for the
   borders.

Make 72   Make 64
for blocks.   for borders.

3. Sew a unit from step 1, four units from step 2,
   and a light/medium 1½" square together to make
   a block. Press as indicated. Make 18 blocks.

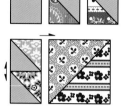 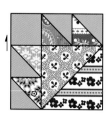

Make 18.

Assembling the Topper

1. Arrange the blocks, side setting triangles, and
   corner setting triangles as shown. Sew the blocks
   and side triangles into diagonal rows. The pink
   triangles are cut oversized and will extend
   beyond the pieced blocks. Sew the rows together
   and add the corner triangles. Trim the table
   topper ¼" outside the block corners.

2 Sew 13 half-square-triangle units together, orienting the triangles in the same direction. Make two units and sew one to the top and one to the bottom of the topper. Sew 19 half-square-triangle units together for each side border. With this many seams, it can be difficult to make the borders exactly the same size as the topper center, so don't worry about fitting everything together perfectly. If a strip is too long, simply cut it off. And if it's too short, add more triangle

units. You can also adjust the lengths by taking a little larger or smaller seam allowance between some of the triangle squares.

Finishing

Go to ShopMartingale.com/HowtoQuilt if you need more information on any of the finishing steps.

1 Layer, baste, and quilt your table topper.

2 Using the brown 2¼"-wide strips, prepare and attach the binding.

Five-Cent Fairy Garden

Even the tiniest scraps from your favorite homespuns, ticking stripes, and plaids can be included in this cheery little quilt. And with one very high-tech gadget—a nickel— you can achieve perfectly shaped berries and flower centers!

FINISHED TOPPER: 21½" x 21½"
Designed and made by Kim Diehl

Materials

Yardage is based on 42"-wide fabric.

½ yard of medium or dark homespun for inner border and binding

40 assorted homespun squares, 1½" x 1½", for quilt center

30 assorted homespun rectangles, 1½" x 2½", for quilt center

4 assorted tan homespun rectangles, 5½" x 11½", for outer border

4 assorted tan homespun squares, 5½" x 5½", for outer border

Assorted homespun scraps for appliqué

Assorted green homespun scraps for appliqué

¾ yard of fabric for backing

27" x 27" piece of batting

Fusible web (optional)

Nickel for appliqué template

⅜" bias bar

Cutting

Appliqué patterns A–H are on page 221. Kim uses freezer-paper appliqué and machine stitching, but you can prepare the shapes for your favorite method. For more details on appliqué, go to ShopMartingale.com/ HowtoQuilt for free information, or see Kim's book Simple Appliqué *(Martingale, 2015) for a variety of appliqué techniques.*

From the ½ yard of medium or dark homespun, cut:
2 strips, 1" x 10½"
2 strips, 1" x 11½"
6 strips, 2½" x 18"

From the assorted homespun scraps, cut:
4 using pattern A
4 using pattern D
4 using pattern E
4 using pattern G
4 using pattern H
24 circles traced with a nickel

From the assorted green homespun scraps, cut:
16 using pattern B
8 using pattern C
4 using pattern F
8 bias strips, 1½" x 10"

Assembling the Topper

Lay out the assorted homespun 1½" squares and the assorted homespun 1½" x 2½" rectangles to form four rows of squares and three rows of rectangles, with 10 pieces in each row. Join the pieces in each row. Press the seam allowances in opposite directions from row to row. Join the rows and press the seam allowances

in one direction. The pieced center should measure 10½" square.

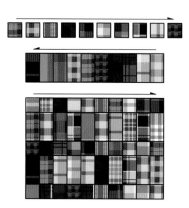

Adding the Borders

1 Join medium or dark homespun 1" x 10½" strips to both sides of the topper center. Press the seam allowances toward the strips. Join 1" x 11½" strips to the top and bottom of the topper center. Press the seam allowances toward the strips.

2 Join tan homespun 5½" x 11½" rectangles to the right and left sides of the topper. Press the seam allowances toward the dark inner-border strips.

3 Join a tan homespun 5½" square to each short end of the two remaining tan rectangles to form a strip. Press the seam allowances toward the squares.

4 Join the pieced border strips to the top and bottom of the topper. Press the seam allowances toward the dark inner-border strips.

Appliquéing the Borders

1 With wrong sides together, fold each green homespun 1½" x 10" strip in half lengthwise and stitch a scant ¼" from the long raw edges to form a tube, then trim the seam allowances to ⅛". Insert the bias bar into the tube and slide it along as you press the stem, making sure the seam is centered and lies flat. Fold under the raw edge at one end about ¼" and use a fabric glue stick to anchor it in place.

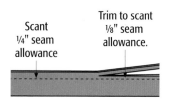

Scant ¼" seam allowance

Trim to scant ⅛" seam allowance.

BIAS-BAR TIP

Whenever a pattern instructs you to sew a fabric tube for use with a bias bar, use a scant ¼" seam allowance. This will allow the bar to move easily through the tube and may eliminate the need to trim the seam allowance.

2 Referring to the photo on page 218 and the diagram below, lay out the appliqués and prepared stems. Begin by appliquéing the pattern C shapes. Then proceed to the 10" stems. As the remaining appliqués are stitched in place, they will cover the unfinished ends of the stems positioned in the corners.

Finishing

Go to ShopMartingale.com/HowtoQuilt if you need more information on any of the finishing steps.

1 Layer, baste, and quilt your table topper.

2 Using the 2½"-wide homespun strips, prepare and attach the binding.

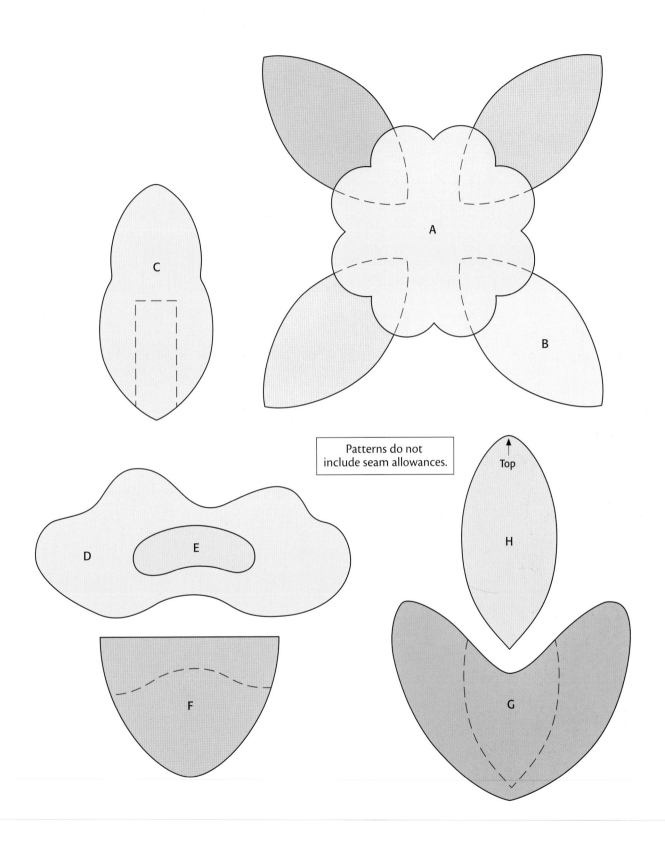

Patterns do not
include seam allowances.

Stella's Baskets

Rickrack stems and perky red appliquéd posies will light up any room year-round, bringing cheer on the chilly days and staying freshly radiant when it's warm.

FINISHED TOPPER: 46½" x 46½"
FINISHED BLOCK: 16" x 16"
Designed and made by Jeanne Large and Shelley Wicks; quilted by Wendy Findlay

Materials
Yardage is based on 42"-wide fabric.

1⅛ yards of cream print for appliqué block backgrounds
1⅛ yards of brown print for sashing, inner border, and outer border
⅝ yard of green print for middle border and binding
¼ yard of red print for stars
12" x 16" piece of brown print for basket appliqués
9" x 10" piece of dark brown fabric for basket rim appliqués
10½" x 11" piece *each* of 3 assorted red prints for flower appliqués
10" x 11" piece of green print for leaf appliqués
7" x 15" piece of gold print for flower-center appliqués
3 yards of fabric for backing
55" x 55" piece of batting
1⅔ yards of ⅝"-wide green rickrack for stems
Fusible web (optional)

Cutting
From the cream print, cut:
2 strips, 16½" x 42"; crosscut into 4 squares, 16½" x 16½"

From the red print, cut:
2 strips, 1½" x 42"; crosscut into 40 squares, 1½" x 1½"
1 strip, 2½" x 42"; crosscut into 5 squares, 2½" x 2½"

From the brown print for sashing and borders, cut:
6 strips, 2½" x 42"; crosscut into:
    4 strips, 2½" x 16½"
    4 strips, 2½" x 34½"
    8 rectangles, 1½" x 2½"
5 strips, 3½" x 42"

From the green print for middle border and binding, cut:
4 strips, 1½" x 42"; crosscut into:
    4 strips, 1½" x 34½"
    4 squares, 1½" x 1½"
5 strips, 2½" x 42"

Appliquéing the Blocks

1 Using the patterns on pages 226 and 227, prepare the shapes for your favorite appliqué method. Jeanne and Shelley used fusible-web appliqué.

2 Using the appliqué placement diagram on page 224 as a guide, trim the rickrack to the desired lengths for stems and pin the stems onto a cream 16½" square. Arrange the prepared appliqué shapes on the square and press in place, being careful not to scorch the rickrack. Use matching thread to sew a straight line down the center of each rickrack stem. Use matching thread

to blanket-stitch around each shape by hand or machine. Repeat to make a total of four blocks.

Appliqué placement

Assembling the Topper

1 Use a pencil and a ruler to lightly draw a diagonal line from corner to corner on the wrong side of each red 1½" square.

2 Layer one of the marked squares over one end of a brown 2½" x 16½" strip as shown, right sides together. Sew from corner to corner directly on the drawn line. Fold the top corner back and align it with the corner of the brown strip beneath it; press. Trim away the excess layers of fabric beneath the top triangle, leaving a ¼" seam allowance. Repeat to make a total of four units. In the same manner, layer a marked red square on the adjacent corner of each strip as shown, and stitch, press, and trim as before to make four star-point units. Set aside the remaining marked 1½" squares.

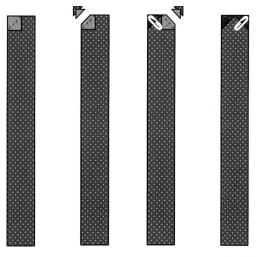

Make 4.

3 Arrange the four star-point units from step 2, one red 2½" square, and the appliquéd blocks into three horizontal rows as shown. Sew the pieces in each row together. Press the seam allowances toward the appliquéd blocks and red square. Sew the rows together. Press the seam allowances toward the block rows.

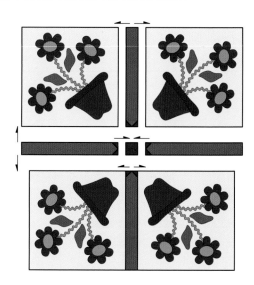

4 Repeat step 2 using the brown 2½" x 34½" strips and the marked red 1½" squares you set aside in step 2, making star points on both ends of the strips. Make four inner-border strips. Set aside the remaining marked 1½" squares.

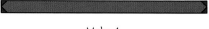

Make 4.

5 Sew inner-border strips to the sides of the table topper. Press the seam allowances toward the table-topper center. Join a red 2½" square to each end of the remaining two inner-border strips. Press the seam allowances toward the squares. Add these strips to the top and bottom of the

table topper. Press the seam allowances toward the table-topper center.

6 Layer one of the remaining marked red 1½" squares over one end of a brown 1½" x 2½" rectangle as shown, right sides together. Sew, press, and trim in the same manner as you did for the star-point units. Repeat to make a total of eight middle-border star-point units.

Make 8.

7 Sew a middle-border star-point unit to each end of a green 1½" x 34½" middle-border strip. Press the seam allowances toward the green strip. Repeat to make a total of four strips.

Make 4.

8 Refer to the assembly diagram at right to sew a middle-border strip to each side of the table-topper top. Press the seam allowances toward the inner border. Sew a green 1½" square to each end

of the two remaining middle-border strips. Press the seam allowances toward the squares. Sew these strips to the top and bottom of the table-topper top. Press the seam allowances toward the inner border.

9 Sew the brown 3½" x 42" outer-border strips together end to end to make one long strip. From this strip, cut two strips, 3½" x 40½", and two strips, 3½" x 46½". Sew the 3½" x 40½" strips to the sides of the table-topper top. Press the seam allowances toward the outer border. Sew the 3½" x 46½" strips to the top and bottom of the table-topper top. Press the seam allowances toward the outer border.

Quilt assembly

Finishing

Go to ShopMartingale.com/HowtoQuilt if you need more information on any of the finishing steps.

1 Layer, baste, and quilt your table topper.

2 Using the green 2½"-wide strips, prepare and attach the binding.

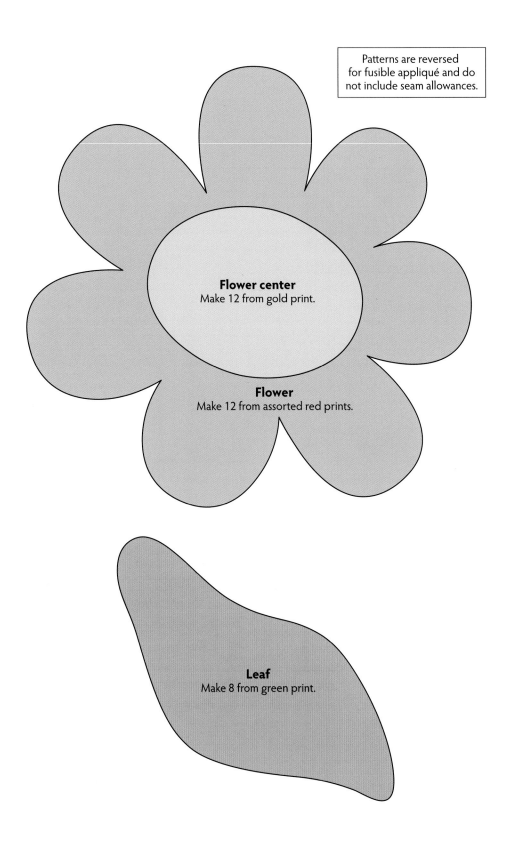

Patterns are reversed
for fusible appliqué and do
not include seam allowances.

Flower center
Make 12 from gold print.

Flower
Make 12 from assorted red prints.

Leaf
Make 8 from green print.

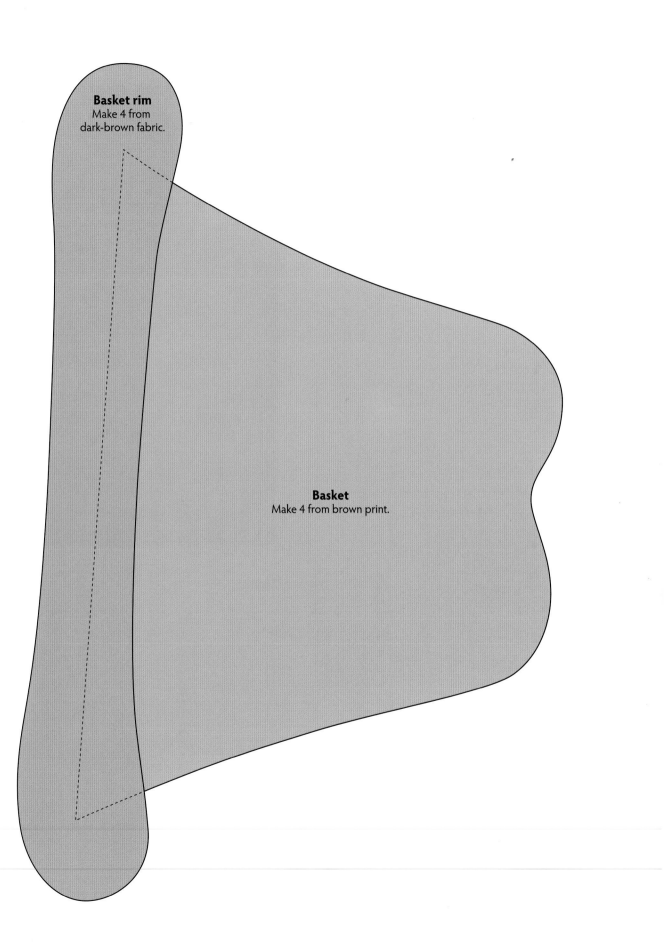

Basket rim
Make 4 from
dark-brown fabric.

Basket
Make 4 from brown print.

Charming Star

When looking at this quilt, you'll find that the pinks and browns take turns dominating what you see. The eyes tend to shift from the star to the diagonal lines of the surrounding blocks. Pink and brown is a classic color combination, but any charm pack with two dominant colors is all you need.

FINISHED TOPPER: 20" x 30"
FINISHED BLOCK: 4" x 4"
Designed and made by Mary Etherington and Connie Tesene

Materials

Yardage is based on 42"-wide fabric. Charm squares are 5" x 5".

14 charm squares of assorted pink prints for blocks and outer border

14 charm squares of assorted brown prints for blocks and outer border

⅓ yard of tan print for blocks and inner border

⅓ yard of pink print for Star block, sashing cornerstones, and border corners

¼ yard of brown print for piecing the Star block, sashing strips, and outer border

¼ yard of a different brown print for binding

¾ yard of fabric for backing

24" x 34" piece of batting

STILL CHARMING

If you don't have a set of precut charm squares, you'll need a 3" x 21" strip *each of* seven pink prints and seven brown prints. In the cutting instructions, double the number of pieces cut from each charm square.

Cutting

When cutting your charm squares, be very careful not to waste any fabric. Measure to the outside of pinked edges. Do not straighten the edges; you'll need every square inch of fabric.

From *each* pink charm square, cut:

2 squares, 1½" x 1½" (28 total)

1 square, 2⅞" x 2⅞" (14 total); cut each square in half diagonally to yield 28 triangles

1 rectangle, 1¾" x 2½" (14 total; 2 will be extra)

From *each* brown charm square, cut:

2 squares, 2½" x 2½" (28 total)

1 rectangle, 2½" x 5" (14 total)

From the tan print, cut:

2 strips 1⅞" x 42"; crosscut into 32 squares, 1⅞" x 1⅞". Cut each square in half diagonally to yield 64 triangles.

4 squares, 1½" x 1½"

3 strips 1½" x 42"; crosscut *1* of the strips into 2 strips, 1½" x 14½", and trim the other 2 strips to 1½" x 26½"

From the pink print, cut:

4 squares, 1⅞" x 1⅞"; cut each square in half diagonally to yield 8 triangles

8 squares, 1½" x 1½"

4 squares, 2½" x 2½"

From the brown print for piecing, cut:

4 squares, 1⅞" x 1⅞"; cut each square in half diagonally to yield 8 triangles

3 strips, 1½" x 42"; crosscut into 22 strips, 1½" x 4½"

2 rectangles, 2½" x 5"

From the brown print for binding, cut:

3 strips, 1½" x 42"

Making the Blocks

Each 4" Charm block is made from one brown charm square, one pink charm square, and the tan print. All four pieces of pink and both pieces of brown print should match within a block. The Star block is not made with charm squares, but with the brown, pink, and tan prints.

1 Place a tan triangle right sides together with a pink charm square, aligning the short edges of the triangle with two sides of the square, and stitch. Press the seam allowances toward the triangle. Sew the short edge of another tan triangle to a side of the pink square as shown. Press toward the triangle. Be careful not to stretch the long side of the tan triangles. Repeat to make two units from each pink charm-square fabric (14 matching pairs).

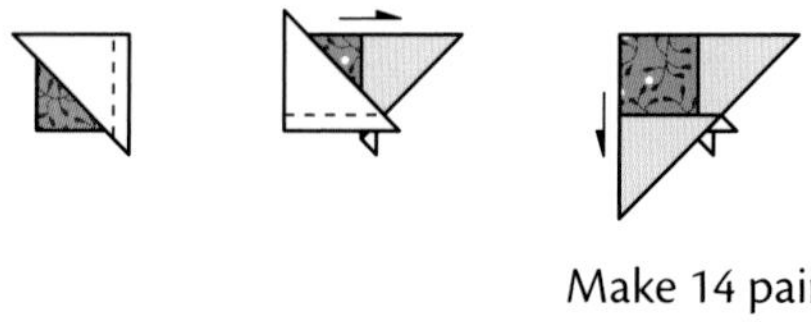

Make 14 pairs.

2 Sew a 2⅞" pink charm triangle to each of the units from step 1, matching fabrics. You will have 14 matching units (28 total).

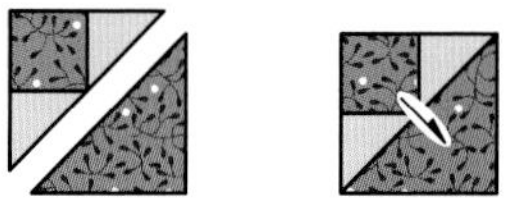

Make 14 matching units.

3 Arrange two matching units from step 2 with two matching brown squares as shown so the pink squares are on the outside of the block. Sew the squares and units together and press. Make 14 Charm blocks.

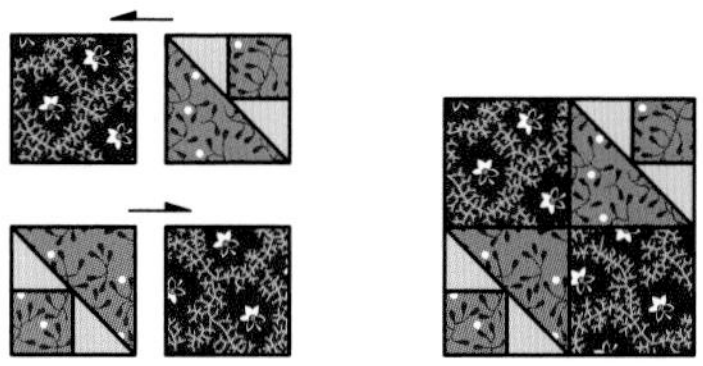

Make 14.

4 For the Star block, sew four pink print 1⅞" triangles to four tan triangles as shown. Sew four brown print triangles to four tan triangles. Sew four pink print triangles to four brown print triangles. Press the seam allowances as shown.

Make 4 of each.

5 Arrange the triangle units from step 4 with four tan 1½" squares as shown. Sew into rows and sew the rows together. It can be difficult to press the seam allowances in a direction that makes it easy to match the points. One solution is to press the seam allowances open instead of to one side.

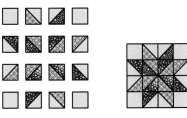

Make 1.

Assembling the Topper

1 Arrange the 14 Charm blocks and the Star block in three columns of five blocks per column with the Star block in the center. In the table topper shown, all of the Charm blocks are oriented in the same direction. Place a brown-print 1½" x 4½" sashing strip between each block. Alternating five sashing strips and four cornerstones as shown, arrange a sashing row between each block row. Sew into rows and sew the rows together. Press toward the sashing strips.

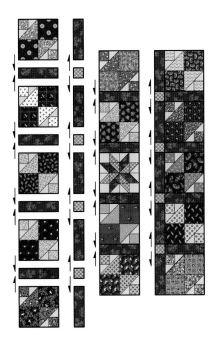

2 For the inner border, sew the tan 1½" x 14½" strips to the top and bottom of the table topper, easing as needed to fit. Sew the tan 1½" x 26½" strips to the sides. Press toward the borders.

3 The outer border is made from the leftover fabrics. Your brown rectangles should measure about 2½" x 5". The 2½" measurement is the border width. If the scraps are a little narrower, trim them all to the narrowest width (either 2¼" or 2"). Trim the pink 1¾" x 2½" rectangles and the four 2½" squares to this same width. For example, if your border pieces are 2¼", cut the pink rectangles 1¾" x 2¼" and the corner squares 2¼" x 2¼".

4 Sew two pink rectangles between three brown rectangles to make a short border. Make two, and check the fit. Borders are too long? Just trim to fit. Borders are too short? Substitute the brown print for one of the rectangles and cut it longer than the others. Sew the borders to the top and bottom of the table topper. Press toward the inner border. Sew four pink rectangles between five brown rectangles to make a long border. Check the fit and add or trim as needed. Sew a pink print corner square to each end. Make two. Sew the borders to the sides of the table topper. Press toward the inner border.

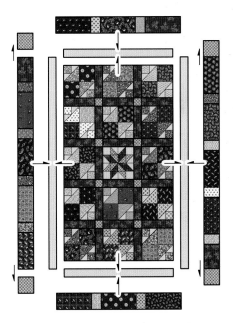

Finishing

Go to ShopMartingale.com/HowtoQuilt if you need more information on any of the finishing steps.

1 Layer, baste, and quilt your table topper.

2 Using the brown 1½"-wide strips, prepare and attach the binding. (Mary and Connie used single-fold binding, not double-fold.)

Basket Weave

All eyes will be on this intriguing tabletop accent—no other centerpiece required. The brown wood and basket fabrics are key to the effect, creating the feeling that you're looking into the center of a woven basket or bowl.

FINISHED TOPPER: 12" x 12"
Designed and made by Connie Kauffman

Materials

Yardage is based on 42"-wide fabric.

⅛ yard of beige print for blocks

⅛ yard of light brown print for blocks

⅛ yard of medium brown print for blocks

⅛ yard of dark brown print for blocks

14" x 14" piece of fabric for backing

14" x 14" piece of batting

Paper for foundation piecing

Cutting

From the dark brown print, cut:

1 square, 2" x 2" (block A, piece 1)

From the beige print, cut:

2 squares, 3" x 3"; cut each square in half diagonally to yield 4 triangles (block A, pieces 34–37)

From the medium brown print, cut:

2 squares, 3" x 3"; cut each square in half diagonally to yield 4 triangles (unit B, piece 1)

Making the Blocks

You can find free downloadable instructions on paper-foundation piecing at ShopMartingale.com/HowtoQuilt.

1 Using the patterns on pages 235 and 236, make one copy of block A, four copies of unit B, and four copies of unit C.

2 Piece the A block as follows:
Dark brown: piece 1
Beige: pieces 2–5, 10–13, 18–21, 26–29, and 34–37
Medium brown: pieces 6–9, 14–17, 22–25, and 30–33

Block A.
Make 1.

3 Piece four B units as follows:
Medium brown: pieces 1, 4, 11, 14, and 21
Light brown: pieces 2, 3, 7, 8, 12, 13, 17, 18, 22, and 23
Dark brown: pieces 5, 6, 9, 10, 15, 16, 19, and 20

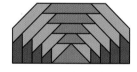

Unit B.
Make 4.

4 Piece four C units using dark brown for piece 1 and light brown for piece 2.

Unit C.
Make 4.

Assembling the Topper

1. Sew B units to opposite sides of the A block to make the center row. Press the seam allowances toward the A block.

2. Sew C units to opposite sides of a B unit as shown to make the top row. Press the seam allowances toward the C units. Repeat to make the bottom row.

Make 2.

3. Join the rows from steps 1 and 2 as shown to complete the table-topper top. Press the seam allowances toward the center. Remove the paper foundations and press.

Table-topper assembly

Finishing

1. Layer the backing right side up on top of the batting. Place the table topper on the backing, wrong side up, and pin around the outside edges.

2. Using a ¼"-wide seam allowance, stitch around the outer edge, leaving a 3" opening on one side for turning.

3. Trim the corners and the excess backing and batting. Turn the table topper right side out through the opening. Press and hand stitch the opening closed.

4. Quilt as desired.

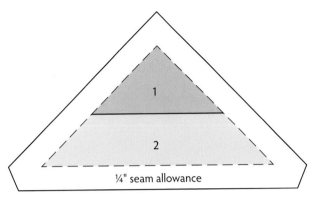

¼" seam allowance

Unit C
Make 4.

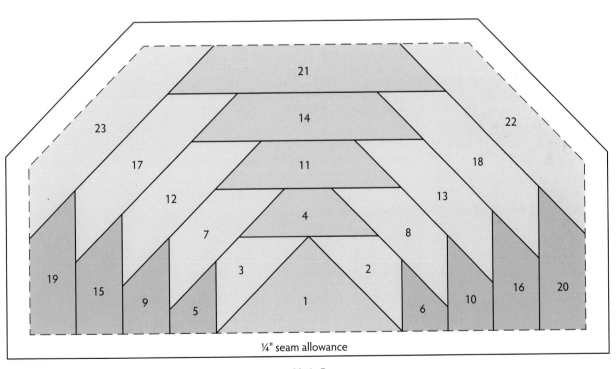

¼" seam allowance

Unit B
Make 4.

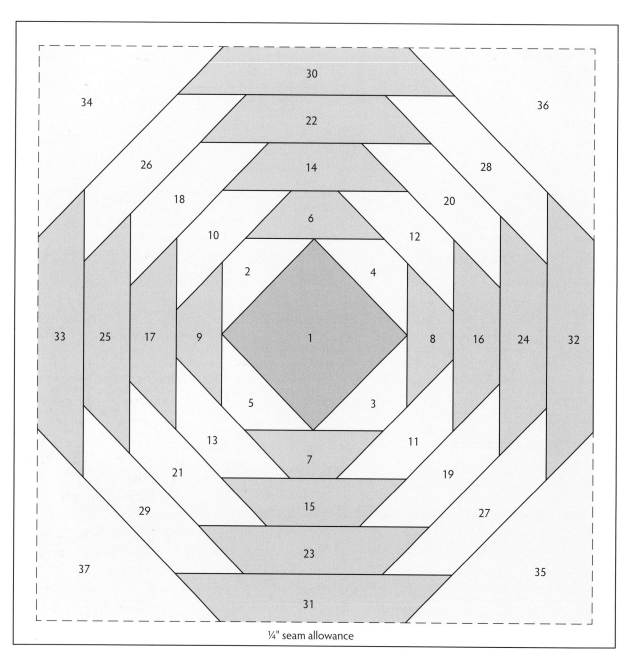

Block A
Make 1.

¼" seam allowance

Snow Happy Family

Who doesn't love a snowman? When winter rolls around, make your home "snow happy" with this quick-to-sew foursome of jaunty gents. Sporting cozy flannel scarves and welcoming grins, they are ready to add instant cheer to any holiday tabletop.

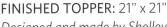

FINISHED TOPPER: 21" x 21"

Designed and made by Shelley Wicks and Jeanne Large; quilted by Jeanne Large

Materials

Yardage is based on 42"-wide fabric. A fat eighth measures 9" x 21".

¾ yard of charcoal flannel for blocks, sashing, and binding

1 fat eighth of white flannel for snowmen

6" x 10" piece *each* of 2 green flannels for scarves and circles

6" x 10" piece *each* of 2 red flannels for scarves and circles

7" x 7" piece of brown flannel for arms

4" x 5" piece of gold flannel for star

2" x 5" piece of orange flannel for noses

1 yard of fabric for backing

29" x 29" piece of batting

Fusible web (optional)

Black embroidery floss and embroidery needle

Cutting

From the charcoal flannel, cut:

1 strip, 9½" x 42"; crosscut into 4 squares, 9½" x 9½"

1 strip, 3" x 42"; crosscut into 4 rectangles, 3" x 9½"

1 square, 3" x 3"

3 strips, 2½" x 42"

Appliquéing the Topper

1. The appliqué patterns are on page 240. Shelley and Jeanne used fusible-web appliqué, but you can prepare the following shapes for your favorite method:

   - 4 snowmen from white flannel
   - 1 scarf, 2 large circles, and 2 small circles from *each* red flannel
   - 1 scarf, 2 large circles, and 2 small circles from *each* green flannel
   - 4 noses from orange flannel
   - 8 arms (4 of each) from brown flannel
   - 1 star from gold flannel

2 Arrange the circles on the charcoal 3" x 9½" rectangles as shown and appliqué in place. Position a snowman, scarf, nose, and two arms on each of the charcoal 9½" squares as shown and appliqué in place. If desired, use a blanket stitch and matching thread to appliqué the edges by hand or machine. Embroider the snowmen's eyes using two strands of floss to make French knots. Embroider the mouths using a running stitch. The star will be appliquéd after the table topper has been put together.

Make 4.

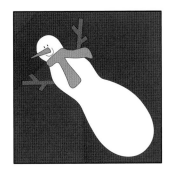

Make 4.

Assembling the Topper

1 Arrange the blocks, sashing, and 3" square in rows as shown. Sew the blocks together into rows, pressing the seam allowances toward the appliquéd sashing. Sew the rows together to form the table topper. Press the seam allowances toward the sashing.

2 Place the gold star in the center and appliqué in place. If you wish, use a blanket stitch and matching thread to appliqué the edges by hand or machine.

Finishing

Go to ShopMartingale.com/HowtoQuilt if you need more information on any of the finishing steps.

1 Layer, baste, and quilt your table topper.

2 Using the charcoal 2½"-wide strips, prepare and attach the binding.

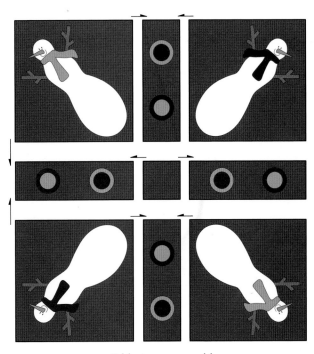

Table-topper assembly

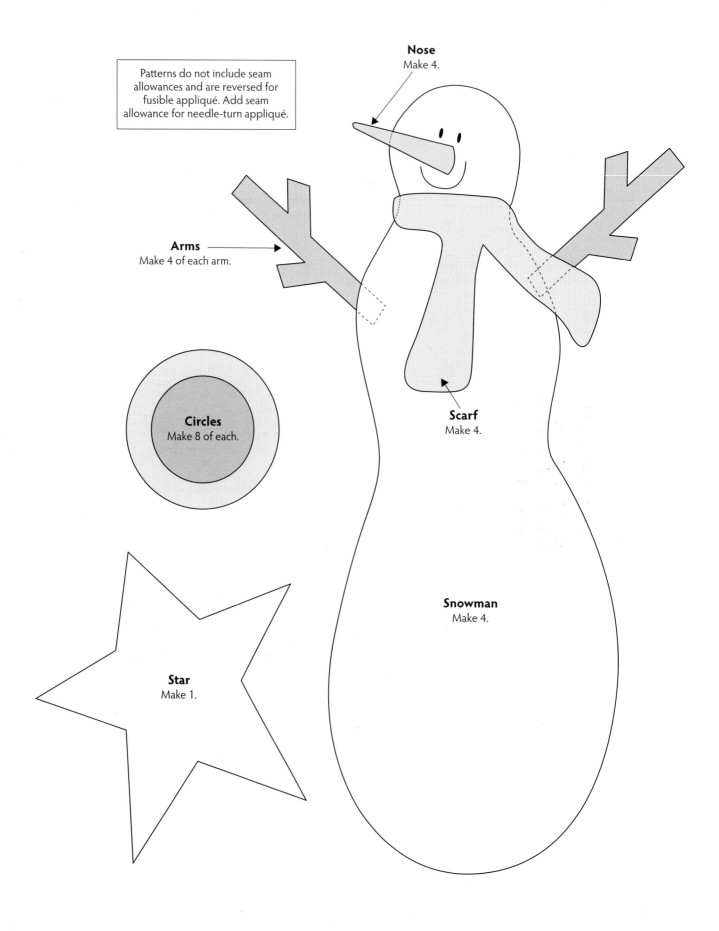

Patterns do not include seam allowances and are reversed for fusible appliqué. Add seam allowance for needle-turn appliqué.

Nose
Make 4.

Arms
Make 4 of each arm.

Circles
Make 8 of each.

Scarf
Make 4.

Star
Make 1.

Snowman
Make 4.